The Language of the Stars

.ll.

WHAT THEY SAY
about Nathan Hellner-Mestelman's first book

COSMIC WONDER
Our Place in the Epic Story of the Universe
(LLP 2024)

"***Cosmic Wonder*** is truly a tour de force."

—*Quill & Quire*

"Imbued with dry-wit humour and a soupçon of existential dread, ***Cosmic Wonder*** manages to be both sobering and reverential as it explores these rich areas of scientific enquiry. This is one up-and-coming writer to watch."

—*Montreal Review of Books*

"Hellner-Mestelman does a good job of putting the reader in the picture, and makes mind-boggling concepts understandable using comparisons. 'If our planet were the size of a blueberry, the distance from the Earth to the Sun would be the length of a football field.'"

—*The Miramichi Reader*

"I definitely felt a huge nostalgic pull while reading this book and was able to excitedly peruse the pages and small illustrations with a fascination that has seemly lain dormant for many, many years."

—*The British Columbia Review*

"An entertaining read that begs to be read at one sitting. I know I had a hard time putting it down."

—Sébastien Décarie

… and readers everywhere: Amazon #1 in YA Astronomy!

The scientific story of a few billion years
in a few hundred pages

Written & illustrated by

Nathan Hellner-Mestelman

.ll.

Published by Linda Leith Publishing, 2025

Edited by Leila Marshy, Kaiya Smith Blackburn.
Cover image and interior illustrations: Nathan Hellner-Mestelman.
Cover design: Debbie Geltner.
Author photo: Park Photo Studio, by Matt Kim

Library and Archives Canada Cataloguing in Publication

Title: The language of the stars: the scientific story of a few billion years in a few hundred pages / written & illustrated by Nathan Hellner-Mestelman.
Names: Hellner-Mestelman, Nathan, author.
Description: Includes bibliographical references.
Identifiers: Canadiana (print) 20240478592 | Canadiana (ebook) 20240485041 | ISBN 9781773901718
(softcover) | ISBN 9781773901732 (PDF) | ISBN 9781773901725 (EPUB)
Subjects: LCSH: Cosmology—Juvenile literature.
Classification: LCC QB983 .H455 2025 | DDC j523.1—dc23

Printed and bound in Canada.

The publisher gratefully acknowledges the support of the Government of Canada through the Canada Council for the Arts, the Canada Book Fund, and of the Government of Quebec through the Société de développement des entreprises culturelles (SODEC).

Linda Leith Publishing
Montreal

Table of Contents

Preface

Nuclear fusion and nerd romance are not commonly two sides of the same coin, but I've been too flabbergasted to ignore the recent allegation that our dating habits are comparable to the proton-proton nuclear chain reaction that powers the Sun in its burning squall. The origin of this theory remains unknown.

At my high school, I attend a program that's quite rigorous on the academic scale, leaving us romantically destitute for a gaping majority of the year. But even so, the rare *affaire de coeur* sometimes befalls us. This previous June, two classmates of mine fell for each other harder than Newton's apple fell for the Earth, and I admit that the theory is true.

The proton-proton chain reaction is a process that burns and bellows in the flaming core of the Sun, at the heart of our solar system. Inside the Sun is a searing ocean of hot ionized plasma that holds positive-charged protons, neutral neutrons, and a hot fray of electrons in a sloshing mix that radiates at the ghastly temperature of 15 million degrees Celsius.

Thanks to their innate positive charge, protons repel each other like magnets. But inside the Sun's core, crushed under the ungodly pressure of 250 billion atmospheres, even protons are shoved within an atom's width of each other—close enough for the *Strong Nuclear Force* to bind them together in a shackling bond that overpowers the petty force of their repulsion by a hundred times. Their atomic embrace is so inseparable that even the

Sun's daily tempest of two quintillion nuclear bombs can't divorce them.

To keep the protons tightly wedded, two neutral-charged neutrons get picked up in the ruckus, leading to a double-proton, double-neutron group that we know as a helium atom.

This whole fiasco releases so much energy that it shoves the surrounding protons and neutrons into their own doubled-up couplets, sustaining the cycle that keeps our Sun passionately roaring each second.

Similar to protons, even we socially repellant nerds can become inextricably bonded under the strong romantic force, provided there's enough peer pressure to helplessly shove us together. To alleviate the

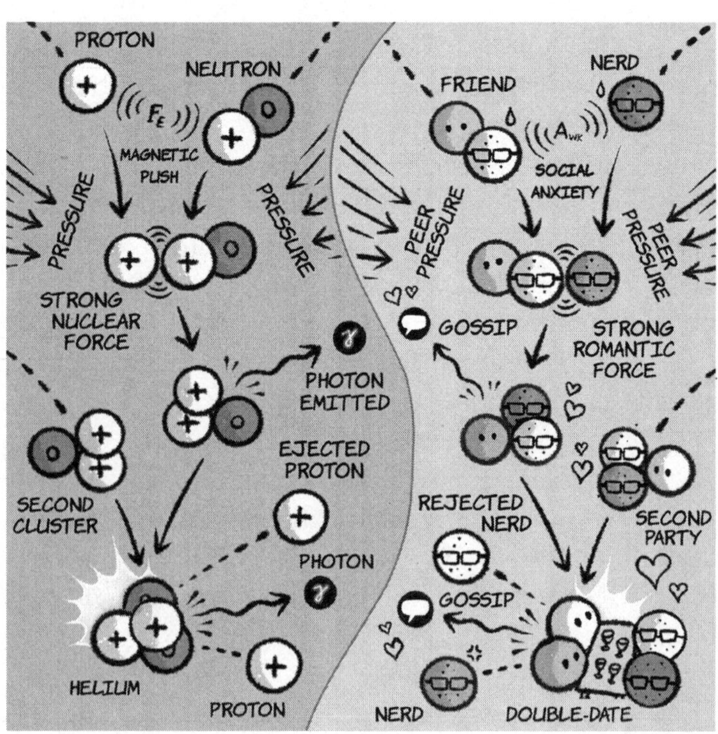

awkwardness, sometimes two non-nerds get picked up, hence the double-date that transpired back in June. The fiasco released such an inordinate amount of gossip that it triggered a whole backwash of prom dates.

Plot it out, and these two phenomena are surely linked.

But corny high-school romantic gossip aside, our cosmos is linked on more levels than we might imagine. There's a common thread between the subtle bond conjoining every atom in the universe, a highway speed limit etched into spacetime itself, an unknown substance weighing six times more than our entire universe, a small household refrigerator, and a recently-invented brand of beer.

After this preface, we shall address the beer first.

This mosaic of natural patterns isn't reserved to outer space. Over the four billion years of life's evolution here on Earth, it has cracked wing-powered flight four discreet times, sound-based echolocation twice, living brains twice, green leafy plants 62 different times, and light-sensitive eyes 65 separate times. Our existence can barely be told apart from the bland patterns that pop up over and over again across the natural world.

You and I, dear reader, already share 99.92% of the genetic code in our cells. No matter how distant your family tree is from mine, our branching roots eventually converge on at least one common ancestor in the last 3,400 years. You are almost guaranteed to be my 50th cousin or closer. If you'll count that as family, all human events you'll ever witness are merely heavily-estranged reunions that sometimes involve guns.

Dial back the clock of evolution, and you'll find 98.8% of our genetic code is shared with our chimpanzee primates, 84% with domesticated dogs, 44% with bananas, and 60% with the mosquitoes you may have

mercilessly swatted last night Those tulip flowers you picked and handed to your date contained 30% human genetics. And you thought it was romantic.

These days, our society seems obsessed with gnawing and chewing apart every detail that makes people different from one another. But underneath our borders, labels and clans lies a slew of scientific common ground. The backstory of our universe—yes, the whole thing—paints that common ground, from its explosive birth to the present moment.

Unfortunately, the entire story is 13.8 billion years long, and my publisher withholds my paper budget from riffling past a few hundred pages, so this book contains an abridged version of the universe—a discount price edition, so to speak.

It doesn't do our universe justice to condense it down into a hundred slices of processed tree splattered and dabbled in ink, but for what it's worth, take this as a tribute to what we've got in common in this complex, beautiful, and awesomely vast cosmos.

Dark Matters of Fact

Our story begins with a trait shared between a recently invented brand of beer and an unknown substance that weighs six times more than all the galaxies in the universe combined. Between these two fungible items, one basic law stands: if something's ubiquitous enough in the natural world, it's going to pop up again, and again, across the universe.

Enter dark matter, an elusive substance that was discovered in an average spiral galaxy containing a small yellow star encircled by an exceptional blue planet with a young and budding intelligent species on its surface. That species discovered a knack for agriculture and soon earned its living on harvesting plants.

Empires climbed and crumbled, and after twelve thousand years of abject civilized chaos, a local beer business called the Hoyne Brewing Company was established in 2011 in a small Canadian city named Victoria. It soon whisked up an alcoholic beverage with flavour notes of chocolate, a beacon that brought my neighbourhood together like fruit flies to a cored apple.

Hoyne named the new drink *Dark Matter*. Each 650 mL bottle holds about 1500 calories, which you might as well consider to be a measurement of dark energy.

Chocolate-tinged beer has a backstory as rich as its industries. Back in 1500 CE, long before Dark Matter ever fermented upon this world, the ancient Aztecs whisked up their own beverage known as *xocolātl*, a bitter mix of cacao pulp and hot spices.

Thanks to traces of fermented cacao that still linger on ancient Mesoamerican pottery, we have archaeological evidence that chocolate, at least in its unprocessed form, might have once been a hugely popular alcoholic beverage in the heyday of the Olmecs and the Mayans in 1400 BCE, a quarter-myriad years before Hoyne ever graced this world.

Beer is so ancient that we could easily use its history to explain our own. All six cradles of civilization—the spawn-points of every major society in the world—discovered the recipe for beer on their own whim. The Sumerians brewed it in 8000 BCE, the Chinese in 7000 BCE, the Egyptians in 6000 BCE, the Indus Valley in 1500 BCE, the Mesoamericans in 1400 BCE, and the Incas in 1500 CE. Beer seems to be a natural checkpoint of civilization, a kind of Rosetta Stone that unites us. Let a culture of humans ferment long enough, and beer will appear.

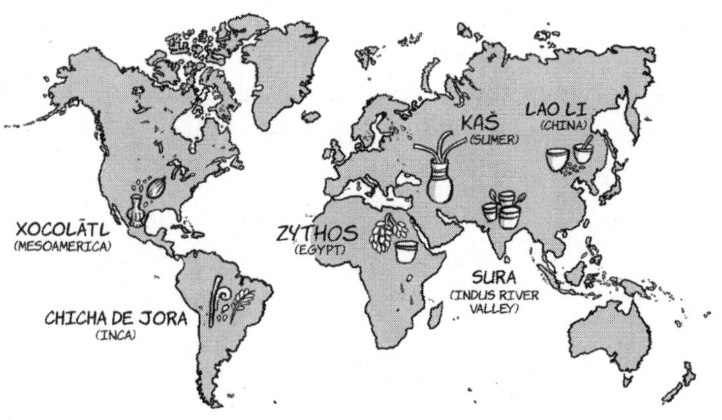

In those ancient times, human civilizations were as distant across the world as isolated planets in a vast universe. We were cast apart by sea-spanning oceans, mountain ranges, and arid deserts. Without a common language spoken between our cultures, the only things we mutually understood were a desperate waddle of hand gestures—and beer, so damn much of it.

The Sumerians, in their expansionist routes, eventually made their first contact with the Egyptians, and from 3500 BCE onward, a trading route ran between their civilizations. Beer was ushered in as a common unit of currency. Jotted on one of the oldest relics of human writing—a clay tablet from 2028 BCE with archaic *cuneiform script* etched into it—are the rations of beer allotted to the Sumerian messengers who first trekked across the desert between two civilizations, two worlds apart.

As societies expanded, we found more than beer in common. Once our ancestors began contemplating the universe around them, we unearthed common ground there too.

If you excavate the ancient relics and scrolls of the Sumerians, the Babylonians, the Chinese, the Egyptians, and the Indus Valley, you'll find one common pattern across them all. You'll be arrested by the *Egyptian Ministry of Tourism and Antiquities*, the *Iraq State Board of Antiquities and Heritage*, the *Archaeological Survey of India*, and the *International Council on Monuments and Sites*. Without a legal excavation licence, the only common thread will be your criminal record.

But with legal permission, one other pattern might stand out to you: one single number was accidentally discovered across all five of these empires. This unifying number, while its discovery might not have been easy as pie, was *pi*.

For the piously unaware, pi is about 3.14, equal to a circle's circumference divided by its width. The Sumerians calculated pi around 2,000 BCE, soon followed by the Egyptians and the Babylonians. Eight hundred years down the line, pi was discovered again during the Yin Dynasty of ancient China. By 600 BCE, even the Indus Valley had spied pi. In our intellectual history, pi seems like just as much a checkpoint as beer.

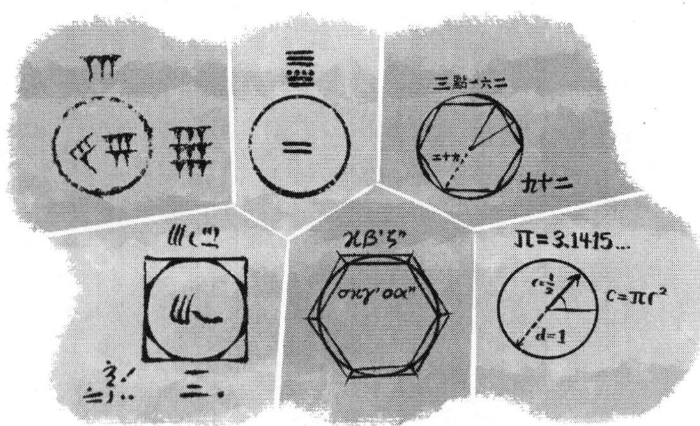

PI: IT COMES FULL CIRCLE

Between those five civilizations, even basic systems of numbers looked almost alien compared to each other. Our modern world runs on a base-10 numeral system that counts up in factors of 10, but there's really nothing special about 10 in math. The Sumerians counted up in factors of twelve; the Babylonians in factors of sixty; the Mayans in factors of twenty; the native Ukomno'm in eight; and the Ndom in six.

But like moths converging to a flame, so many of these cultures discovered pi like a piece of cake. That's the universal beauty of mathematics. If it counts, it works.

Our discovery of pi marked our first smidge of fluency in the odd language of nature. It's a lingo that we've only been dabbling in for a few millennia, but it's one that all human societies in the world—and quite possibly all brainiac civilizations in the known universe—might speak in common. Fast-forward two millennia, and we found patterns embedded in the cosmos itself.

Chocolate-tinged beer, by a truly awesome coincidence, embellished the menu at several astronomy conferences in the wake of the *2003 Breakthrough of the Year* convention, a summit that celebrated one of the world's most profound discoveries on a vast and invisible substance that fills our universe: dark matter—the cosmic kind.

That discovery was made thanks to a team of astronomers using the WMAP satellite (the Wilkinson Microwave Anisotropy Probe), launched into orbit two years earlier. Adorned with its telescopic eyes, the satellite clicked a snapshot of our universe when it was a mere 380,000 years old, way back when space still radiated with the echo of the Big Bang itself—a dim smattering of microwaves known as Cosmic Microwave Background.

Back in those olden *days*, our universe was rolling in a teenaged tempest of thick plasma. That tempest soon collapsed into a dense cluster of stars and galaxies, but its collapse demanded a pull from gravity—one *mighty hell* of a pull indeed.

When the WMAP data stacked up, every ounce of matter in the entire universe gave only 15% of the oomph needed to pull our cosmos together. The remaining 85% of that oomph was missing, or came from something totally invisible. So we came to realize, to our excitement and mild dread, that six-sevenths of the universe is a complete mystery.

It's known as dark matter, and much like the beer brand, it's not a lightweight. But there's some key differences I feel obliged to highlight. Despite sharing the name, Dark Matter beer is well-understood by astronomers, it's visible and touchable, and unless you're at an endless hell-off-its-rockers party, you're not swimming in it every second of your life. The opposite is true for dark matter, the cosmic substance.

With drinks set aside, we've known something dark was brewing since 1933, when the astronomer Fritz Zwicky noticed that the distant *Coma Cluster* of galaxies should be exploding. Even with its galaxies rocketing around each other at absurd speeds, they remain attached by a gravitational pull—a pull that is 10 times stronger than the cluster's small stash of matter would suggest. Dark matter holds the rest.

Fast-forward to 1978, the astronomer Vera Rubin measured 21 spinning spiral galaxies, not too different from our own. Her results stood out because of how furiously fast those galaxies were spinning. Like a festive merry-go-round on overdrive mode, the stars on the fringes of these galaxies should have been slingshotted off their spiral arms and launched into the void of space.

Our own solar system orbits in this high-speed danger zone in the Milky Way galaxy, and since we obviously haven't been tossed into deep space like a ping pong ball, Rubin established the notion that something dark and massive binds these galaxies together.

But the greatest thing about dark matter is its oldness. Thanks to its telltale pull on the distant radiation of the Cosmic Microwave Background, we turned the WMAP satellite into a timekeeper in 2003 to pinpoint, to a tee, the birthdate of our universe: 13.8 billion years ago.

And this brings us to our first universal pattern.

Dark matter is literally everywhere, looming over the cosmos like oxygen over this planet or social anxiety over teenagers. It silently seeps through billions of planets and galaxies without touching a single atom.

Anyone in the universe, no matter where, should witness its subtle effects on the Cosmic Microwave Background. If an extraterrestrial species were curious, they could even pinpoint the exact same 13.8-billion-year cosmic history we did, and that age could serve as a common time-reference clock if we ever chose to communicate across the chasm of space.

If we make contact with alien life, our kinship probably won't be through starships or fringe pop culture or psychic rituals; it'll come from a basic understanding of nature. Just like we humans historically bonded over beer, the whole universe might bond over a shared nerdom of what makes the cosmos tick.

But to *really* see what we've got in common with the rest of the cosmos, we need to dial back the clocks—before clocks, before tools, before the dawn of humankind, before our distant ancestors ever had the audacity to start climbing trees, before life ever decorated this blue planet, before the Earth existed, right back to the moment space and time began.

Agents of Chaos

Hold up for one hot second. Before we kickstart the universe and spend the next fifty-or-so pages talking about the absolute mayhem that went down over the 13.8 billion years leading right to our existence, let's address a crucial rule in our cosmos—a law of physics that's followed by literally everything, from human beings to plants to bacteria, and even, as we'll soon see, to kitchen fridges.

All objects in existence, from atoms to galaxies, have one common trait, and that is their habit of making a godawful, bedraggled mess of this universe. Everything tends toward a state of chaos and disorder thanks to this one law known as *entropy*—and that's where we start our story, since the entire history of our cosmos would be lacking without first pointing out what's really driving it all. It's thanks to entropy that galaxies arose, stars appeared, planets lumped together, life evolved, and we humans got a chance to exist.

To dutifully spoil the remainder of this book, I'll disclose that our universe started off in a state of total cleanliness and order; the Big Bang was the ultimate high point in janitorial history, and it's been getting worse ever since. Clouds of gas stirred up into stars, hotspots cooled down, stars exploded, planets lumped and crumbled, life arose and rotted, and overall, the cosmos went from a spotless canvas of plasma to looking like a teenager's room—and we're so lucky it did.

Entropy is the reason that wood ignites and burns into charcoal, but charcoal doesn't ever freeze back into cold wood. It's the reason sugar cubes dissolve in hot coffee, but don't ever stir themselves back into cubes. It's the reason coffee cools down, never to be hot again; coffee mugs shatter, never to be mugs again; broken bits disintegrate, never to be mugs again. For its entire life, our universe has been swirling itself into a messier place, and entropy has been getting worse.

Nothing in the universe actually *wants* or *desires* to be disordered; it's a result of random chance. Think of our cosmos as a Rubik's Cube. There's just *one* solved position a Rubik's Cube can be in, but there's 43.25 quintillion messy positions to scramble it into. With each random twist, you're ridiculously more likely to make the cube messier than you are to solve it.

Our universe is always twisting at random, so the odds are pretty horribly stacked against your room re-organizing, your sugar cubes re-materializing in coffee, or a heap of broken glass clinking back together into a coffee cup.

It's not that messes can't be cleaned; it's just that the *action* of cleaning them up creates a bigger mess. I can clean my room, sure, but in the action of cleaning it, the energy I burn creates a worse mess than the one I'm solving. Food gets digested, heat is dissipated, and the messiness of our cosmos, overall, doesn't budge backward.

But if messes can't get better, how the star-studded heck did a bunch of unkempt plasma, over 13.8 billion years ago, slowly rearrange itself into a galaxy, a solar system, a planet, a bunch of cells, and eventually into a neat, intricate human brain, hard-wired with 80 billion nerve cells, currently reading a sentence about itself?

This is where, as a fitting metaphor, we invoke a kitchen fridge.

Kitchen fridges, thanks to the law of entropy, actually make things *hotter*. If you're trying to freeze a litre of water, it'll cost your electricity bill about 320,000 joules of energy. But that's hot power right there—enough to *melt* four litres of ice to room temperature.

So by freezing water, you dump about *four times* more heat into the world than the cold you've created. The only task that a fridge really accomplishes is taking the entropic mess *out* of the ice and dumping it somewhere else—in this case, into the environment in the form of wasted electrical heat that you're never getting back.

You might be pondering, at this point, how a kitchen fridge has anything to do with the cosmos or life or anything. But here's what fridges have in common with life: both are possible because the mess of entropy can undo itself in small places, creating order—but at the expense of a crapload of energy, scrambling the rest of the world and making a bigger mess elsewhere.

Our universe has done this over its history, again and again, stirring up finer and finer details while at the same time trashing the overall state of the cosmos at large. It's how stars first arose, life evolved, and we came to exist—and it's what'll eventually kill us all.

Entropy really is the one law that we're all bound by. Take a look at our entire planet. It's showered in light from the Sun, soaking it up like a sponge and becoming warmer. At the same time, Earth radiates heat and light back into space, sweating off that energy and cooling down.

The Sun shines on the Earth with high-energy visible light, while the Earth emits a feeble trickle of low-energy infrared light back into space. Earth doesn't create or destroy any sunlight; it just absorbs the bright energy of our Sun and smothers it into wasted heat. For every *one* bright photon of sunlight that strikes us, Earth spits about 20 dim infrared photons back.

Earth is just as bound by entropy as the rest of the universe.

Our planet is awesome at soaking up hot energy and converting it into useless waste heat. But life, as it turns out, is far better. Thanks to all that food being eaten, those calories burning, and compost rotting, life's existence makes our Earth smear out about 26% *more* sunlight than an alternate Earth with no life, accelerating its entropic mess even more.

The pages of this book are made of cellulose harvested from a tree that once grew thanks to the energy of the Sun—about 8,000,000 joules of it, to be exact: the equivalent of sun-tanning for seven hours, all wrangled up in these pages. Burn this book, and those 8,000,000 joules of stored-up solar energy will be liberated in a blazing fire, leaving nothing behind but a pile of ashes, a bunch of wasted heat, an entropic mess, and a very dismayed author.

Perhaps life is a natural checkpoint of our universe as it falls deeper into its pit of entropy. Gas clouds lumped into stars, stars stirred up planets, and at least once in our universe, a planet spawned life. Chemistry coagulated into cells, cells lumped into colonies, colonies fused into complex creatures, and on every level of that cosmic food chain, atoms got better and better at smearing out heat in a manner that was as disorganized as possible.

Somewhere along that hierarchy of messiness, atoms became so well-organized that, in a weird kind of brainy awareness, they started to think about their own existence.

Entropy is a universal law, so physics, chemistry, and all of nature's rulebooks tend to act the same no matter where you're based. It's no surprise that life evolved so many common traits over its history; nature is locked and predisposed to follow whatever path requires the least effort and energy—and that stirs up all kinds of patterns.

Take the rain, for example.

The Earth holds about a septillion kilograms of water, which gets tossed around, boiled away off the oceans, whisked up into clouds, and dumped back to the ground as rain. Even on the glacial –180°C landscape of Saturn's moon Titan, liquid methane trickles in the same patterns that water follows on Earth, pouring down as methane rain.

Upon the hellish lava-licked 3,000°C surface of the planet K2-141b—a horrific world we spotted over 200 light-years away—rain does fall, though it's molten rock. Rain falls on Venus in a caustic mix of sulphuric acid; it falls as ammonium on Jupiter, crystallized carbon on Uranus, and even as a torrential downpour of plasma on the Sun's surface. Rainfall is just a bunch of potential energy being released; it's no surprise it happens everywhere.

Over our universe's history, we're greeted with a full platter of patterns—from the very particles that make us, our atoms, the molecules in our cells, the letters in our genetic code, the traits we evolved, and at the bottom of it all, the guidelines of entropy. To watch it unfold, it's time to start the clocks and let this story begin—for real this time. With that, welcome to the universe.

Born from the Same Bang

No guests attended the inaugural birthday of our universe, which is a huge shame because it was a real banger of a celebration. Around 13.8 billion years down memory lane, in the middle of nowhere, a quantum ripple set in motion a symphony of physics that exploded our universe into existence. Poof, there it was.

That introduction might have sounded a bit shallow, because even though we've mapped out a huge swath of our universe's history *after* the Big Bang occurred, our scientific knowledge simply tanks like a deflating submarine when it comes to explaining the very moment of cosmic creation. Space is far too glitched up.

The fabric of space behaves like a froth, sloshing in an ocean of bubbling particles called the quantum foam. This subatomic sea ripples at the scale of about 10^{-35} metres, a hundred-billion-trillion-trillion times smaller than this book, as ridiculously small compared to one grain of sand as a grain of sand is compared to the entire observable universe. This distance, known as the Planck Length, is the limit of smallness in our known universe. Try to shrink smaller, and our rigid laws of physics get lost in the messy bubbling foam of space itself.

So before the fresh young age of 10^{-43} seconds, two million-trillion-trillion-trillionths of an eye-blink after time began, our whole universe was stuck in this bubbling foam, even smaller than the Planck Length, like a movie shrunk smaller than a pixel on a screen. This is a chapter of cosmic history still beckoning to be explored.

And then space had a gut-wrenching growth spirt. Puberty is a charming experience that even our universe endured when it was around 10^{-36} seconds old. During that moment, space frantically grew in size 100 septillion times, inflating from a blueberry-sized bubble to the size of our galactic supercluster in a snap.

The physicist Alan Guth, who pioneered research on the Big Bang, developed the field of *cosmic inflation* in 1979 to explain our universe's explosive teenage nanoseconds. After a rough adolescence lasting around 10^{-32} seconds, our universe's expansion halted in an instant. This was not a gentle stop, more like a supersonic bus hitting the brakes at Mach seven and then Tokyo-drifting into a brick wall.

All the energy that drove our universe's cosmic inflation was now converted to pure heat. In a sickening explosion, our universe soared to the ungodly temperature of 10 nonillion degrees Celsius—only a tad bit harsher than California in the summertime—so indescribably hot that a cacophony of particles burst into existence across the universe like cosmic popcorn. Trillions of quarks and electrons, born fresh in this soupy inferno, filled our universe.

You, as a collection of matter, began here.

Most of this matter was about to be tossed down the drain and obliterated, but for a split-second of fleeting stability, our entire universe hung suspended in a bizarre kind of bond known as quantum entanglement.

In the maddening realm of quantum mechanics, whenever two particles get close enough to interact, their properties rub off on each other like two peas in a subatomic pod. Check in on one, and you'll instantly determine the state of the other. If one's spinning upward, you'll know in a pinch that its twin is spinning downward. Drag those twins a universe's distance apart, and they'll still be connected—they'll be quantum entangled.

Our cosmos exploded in such a tight-knit packet that particles from all corners of space influenced each other, linking up a net of entangled particles that spanned the entire universe. In the maddening rush of our expanding universe, space stretched out, wafting those particles away from each other. But their coupled-up links never vanished.

Choose any particle in your body, and chances are it's entangled to a handful of others scattered across the universe.

This may sound absurd—and granted, since it's quantum, you'd have to be bonkers *not* to call it absurd—but a quark in your left nostril could be twinning with a quark blowing in the lofty sand dunes of a planet on the other end of the universe. And if, by some chance, you're coupled up with a human being via some mutual affection, there's about a 1-in-10^{40} chance that one of your particles was paired up with one of theirs in the frenzy of the Big Bang.

Next came an epic obliteration of our entire universe, almost.

Our universe loves balancing out. If you attempt to whisk up matter from thin air, you'll get a side entrée of equally-and-oppositely charged *antimatter* to balance it out. Create a quark, and you'll get an antiquark too. Cook up some positive protons, and you'll get a fresh batch of negative antiprotons to cancel them out. This basic symmetry, known as *charge-parity*, is a fundamental rule of our cosmos. Create a universe, and you'll get an anti-universe served on the same platter. Put matter and antimatter together, and they'll annihilate each other, exploding violently like spiteful siblings.

And that's the shenanigans that unfurled, all at once, in our fresh universe. In the worst knockout battle in cosmic history, about 10^{90} quarks and 10^{90} antiquarks came into existence, greeted one another, then suddenly exploded. To put all that in perspective, this is five billion universes worth of matter, all gone in an instant. In an eye-shattering flash, the entire universe cancelled itself out.

Except, it clearly missed some, because we still exist.

Oddly enough, this single question is still one of the greatest unsolved queries of science: why the heck does our universe still exist? It's been called *baryogenesis* as a working title, but in truth, there's not enough evidence to pin down what cooked up that *slight* extra serving of matter *without* a complimentary side dish of antimatter to cancel it.

What could have brewed all this extra matter?

Some clarity arrived in 2020—a year that was mostly defined by a total lack of it—when the Large Hadron Collider's LHCb detector studied the odd habits of an oddball particle called a B-meson. It tends to decay into matter 55% of the time, picking antimatter only 45% in contrast. With that gobsmacked bias toward matter, we might owe that fallout of extra matter to a crowd of B-mesons at the beginning of the universe.

Whatever went down, only about 1 in 1.6 billion matter particles survived the hullabaloo of our universe's explosive birth. Those leftover particles went onward to create every planet and galaxy, every star and nebula, every moon and asteroid, and every living creature in our entire universe. Your particles were all among the 0.000 000 000 63% who made it.

After about one second had ticked past, the universe had cooled down to the reasonable and temperate heat of 10 trillion degrees Celsius, letting the surviving quarks huddle in tight-knit triplets, giving rise to the first protons and neutrons.

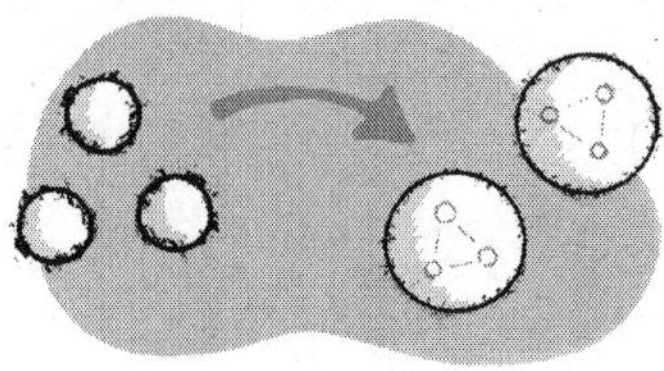

Three minutes later, our cosmos baked at the modest sauna of 10 billion degrees Celsius. The protons and neutrons were cold enough to bond together into the first nuclei of hydrogen and helium, but as we know, protons simply despised their company, so it took the ironclad embrace of the Strong Nuclear Force to squeeze them into nuclear families.

After the first nuclei appeared in our universe, a thick plasma settled in. It was a dark and stormy nightmarish plasmic hell, so crammed with frantic particles that light ricocheted back and forth in all directions. While protons and neutrons had bonded, electrons still zipped around carefree for another 380,000 years until the universe finally chilled enough for the plasma to freeze. Once the temperature dipped down under 10,000°C, atoms settled all at once—protons and neutrons and electrons and all.

Ever since then, matter has been chained up in the shackling cuffs of the Strong Nuclear Force, which leaves us in a freakishly empty universe. Only a hundred-billion-trillion-trillionth of our universe's total volume is occupied by atoms. About a ten-trillionth of the space inside atoms is actually filled up by protons and neutrons, which are huddled up sweet in the dense and cramped atomic nucleus. Just a trillionth of the space inside protons and neutrons is occupied by quarks, wedded in their tiny triplet groups. The rest is, truth be told, a void.

The one trait we humans really share, by a mind-boggling ratio of 99.999999999999999999999996%, is nothingness. Your mass comes almost entirely from the forces holding your atoms together, not the atoms themselves. So if you ever get the feeling that we have nothing in common, you're absolutely correct.

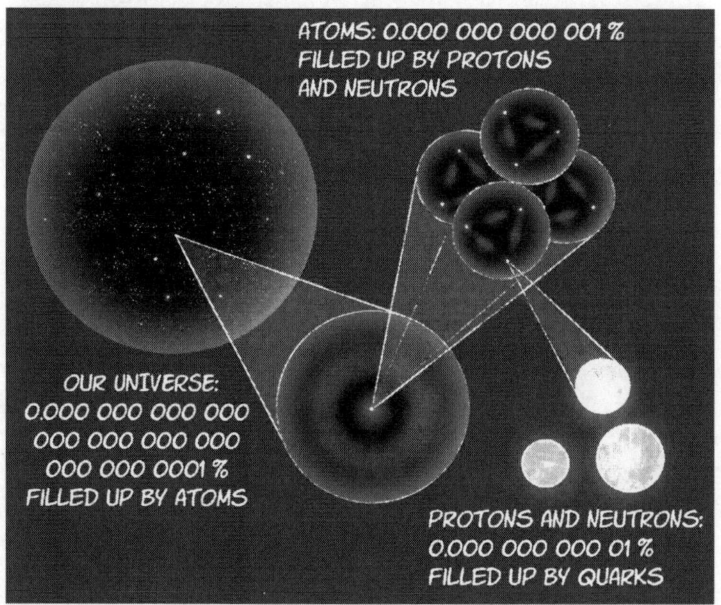

Our universe, 380,000 years after the clock started, was a neatly-blended smoothie of hot hydrogen and helium gas. With atoms finally settled, light waves could shine across the cosmos without being scattered by free-flying electrons. For the first time ever, the universe glowed with light—a hellish cosmic tanning salon filled with X-rays and gamma rays. And almost 14 billion years later, as those rays gradually faded into dim microwaves, it was picked up in the small robotic eyes of a camera built by the ape-descended critters of one small blue planet. In 2003, the WMAP satellite showed us this cosmic masterpiece firsthand.

By now, our universe was a smoothie of pure hydrogen and helium—and like a lukewarm pond of water, this smoothie was close to 99.999% evenly-spread in a balmy hydrogenous soup. But somehow, in the relatively speedy span of 100 million years, that soup pulled itself together into an eclectic hot-spotted ocean of stars. Regular matter wasn't heavy enough to hoist the soup together alone; it took a behemoth that was six times heavier.

So, dark matter arguably mattered even more.

Lighting Up the Universe

The Big Bang was finished so quickly you could've timed it with a stopwatch. But the universe's encore show dragged onward for millions and billions of years.

Our small 3.1 pound ape-descended brains can't picture that; our minds tick in hours and minutes, not eras and eons. So rather than imploding our minds in a futile attempt to picture billions of years, let's switch our timescales completely.

Back in 1977, the astronomer Carl Sagan imagined squeezing the entire age of our universe into a single year, with January 1st marking the Big Bang, and December 31st leading up to this exact moment in time—a kind of cosmic birthday. Although Sagan never lived to see his idea become a blockbuster film series on National Geographic, he would've celebrated his 90th birthday this year. So to put our universe in perspective, let's talk about birthdays.

We're familiar with using years. It takes 365 days for the Earth to encircle the Sun, and to honour this, humans often engage in a ritual that involves blowing the microbiome of one's mouth onto a fresh-baked loaf of candle-lit bread, which guests then devour. But there's a second birthday we could celebrate on a far grander scale. Our entire solar system hurtles around the Milky Way galaxy, completing a full orbit every 225 million years.

In other words, what if we measured time with *galactic birthdays* instead?

On this timescale, a single galactic birthday crosses 225 million of Earth's years; and we'd only have to wait around 0.06 galactic birthdays—less than 10 million of Earth's years—until the cosmos settled to a comfortable temperature, and space was pleasant. Kind of.

On its transition from a deadly sauna to a frosted freezer, the cosmos once passed through a pleasant, even summer-vacation-worthy temperature zone. In 2014, physicist Abraham Loeb calculated that after 10 million years, space had dropped below 100°C, and just five million years later, it marinated at 25°C, about as warm as your average New York springtime afternoon. That means our universe, for a brief little golden age, could have sported liquid water on anything that could hold it.

Whenever you shout *liquid water*, biologists squeal in an inexplicable fit of excitement. Water is the hallmark breeding ground for life as we know it, and who wouldn't be excited about the idea of life spawning a mere tick after time began, basking in the lukewarm afterbirth of our universe? With a bit of luck, in that lustrous age of the cosmos, water might have thawed into the puddles needed to kickstart life. No need for stars, since space *itself* provided the warmth. As our universe cooled off, those puddles might have frozen into rocks and asteroids—museums of the earliest fossils in cosmic history—or not. For now, we can only speculate.

Eventually, about 17 million years after the Big Bang, our universe crossed the 0°C line and froze forever, tending toward the horrific −270°C it sits at nowadays. Fast-forward about 100 million years and the first stars began to shine, about five galactic months after the Big Bang.

Guided with massive blobs of dark matter, huge nebulas of gas collapsed under gravity like marbles welling up into the centre of a trampoline, crushing denser until atoms fused and exploded into blazing balls of plasma.

Nebulas are like cosmic rainclouds, and stars are their raindrops.

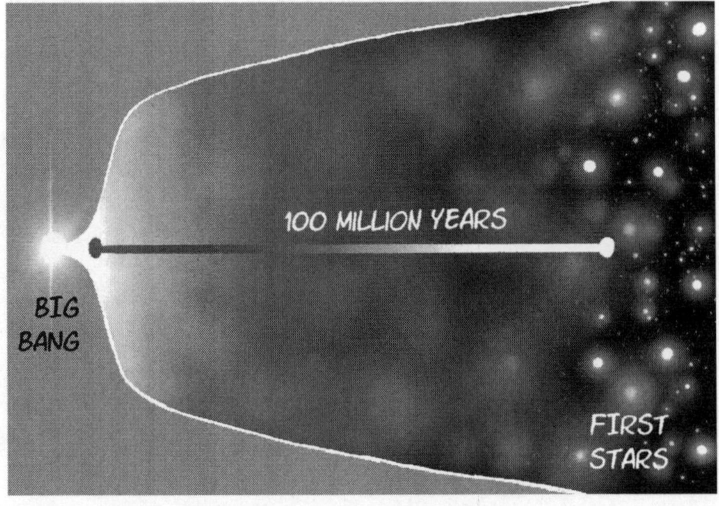

Most of these first-generation stars were extremely hot, intensely bright, and short-lived. They opted for the notorious "*party hard, die young!*" mentality, burning up to 200 times heavier, 20 times hotter, and 30 million times brighter than the Sun, but burning for only 0.05% as long. In a ferocious squall, our universe cooked up 95% of all the stars that *will ever* be born. It's all been a bit of a sober afterparty from that point onward.

Those first stars cooked so screamingly hot that they slammed hydrogen into far heavier atoms. In the same proton-proton chain reaction that pins the romantic gossip in my high school, these stars guzzled up the universe's plain hydrogen smoothie and spiced it into a delectable blend of carbon, nitrogen, magnesium, phosphorous, and even deadweight iron. The bouquet of elements in your body were forged here.

Once enough heavy iron was lugging around inside the cores of the first stars, they went out with a bang, collapsing under gravity and blowing themselves up in supernova explosions. These celestial bombshells packed such an unimaginable punch that even the deadweight iron got smashed into iodine, gold, tungsten, silver, uranium, plutonium, and so much more.

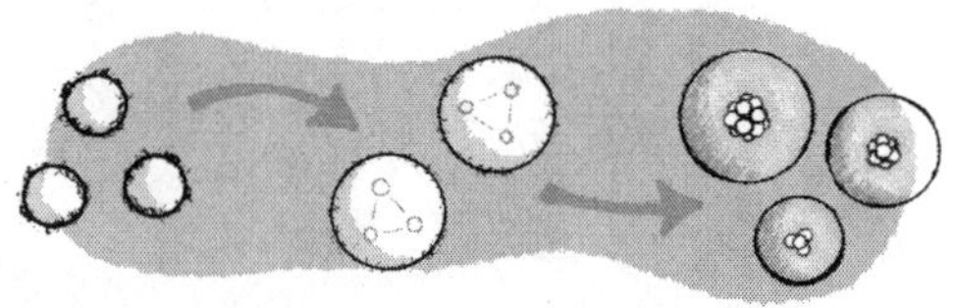

Despite being so powerful, the Big Bang only managed to create hydrogen, helium, and a tiny smidge of lithium. Everything else was cooked in stars. The carbon in pencils, the oxygen in your breath, the phosphorous in matchsticks, the iodine in cooking salt, the copper in brass, the silver in tooth-fillings, the tin in soda cans—all of it was forged in the nuclear factories we like to call stars. To see those factories in action, all you need to do is look up under a clear sky. Night or day, you'll be able to see at least one.

The Spiral Starcase

Our next chapter of cosmic history was paved by devious little things that smash the rules of our universe to pieces. But first, a note about the highway speed limit.

Get in the car and floor down the pedal, full throttle. What's the speediest velocity you can reach? Chances are it's the highway speed limit—which, in British Columbia, rarely exceeds 120 kilometres an hour. Toss away those laws, and with enough horsepower and willpower, your car could probably manage 180, maybe 200 per hour.

Ditch the car, strap a jetpack on, and your human body could stand about 2,500 to 3,000 kilometres an hour before the wind-whipped force of the air against your face crushed you dead. Get in a spacesuit, jump in a rocket, and once you booked about 40,000 km/h, you'd break free the gravitational embrace of Earth completely, launch into space, and never return.

But even then, our universe comes with its *own* interstate highway speed limit that seems to be quite impossible to break—and we've known about it for over three centuries.

In 1610, the new astronomer on the block was Galileo Galilei. He aimed his telescope at Jupiter and recognized, in an instant, four pinpointed moons dancing around it. This was the first time in history that we'd ever seen objects *not* orbiting Earth, but another world.

Galileo was a hardcore astronomer with a level of obsession that rivals even the most die-hard scientists.

For months he watched those four moons circle around Jupiter, mapping their positions each night with rigour.

He noticed in particular that Io, the innermost moon, ran like clockwork, casting a routine shadow on Jupiter every 42 hours and 27 minutes without ever missing a beat.

By 1676, the Dutch astronomer Ole Rømer noticed that Io was failing its shadow routine. When the Earth passed closest to Jupiter, the shadow of Io came nine minutes too early. Six months later, it arrived nine minutes late. How could a moon, literally the most predictable object in the universe, be as off-schedule as a New York subway train?

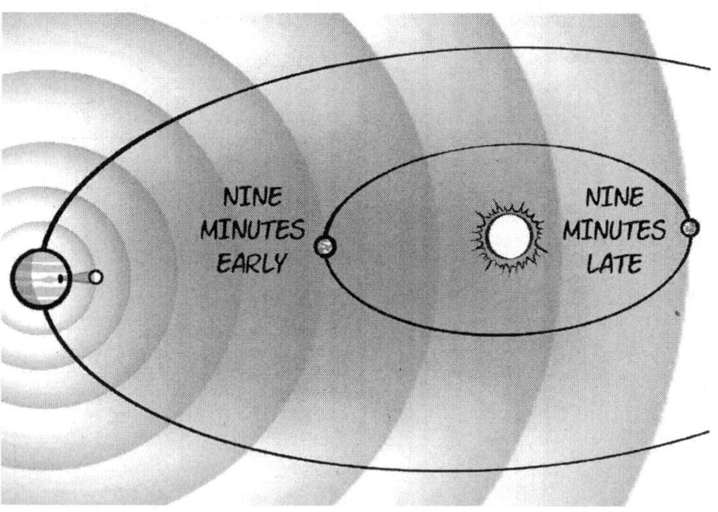

When Rømer plotted it out, he realized it wasn't *Io* that arrived off-schedule, but the *light rays* of Io and its shadow. When we passed closest to Jupiter, its light had a shorter distance to cross. Furthest away from Jupiter, the voyage of Io's light was lengthened by 18 minutes, and we witnessed the spectacle much later.

In the same way you'll hear a sound delay when standing a mile from a music concert, you'll see a light delay in the vastness of the cosmos. And because of that light delay, we came to realize that space comes with a speed limit.

Light is a hardcore speed limit, barring anything from exceeding 299,792,458 metres per second on the dot. Impossible to exceed, horribly expensive to approach, and borderline illegal to even try—it's got all the properties of a highway speed limit. Cosmic laws apply everywhere; no matter where you are, light-speed is light-speed.

Attempt to break this limit, and a) you'd probably be arrested, handed a 2.6-billion-dollar speeding ticket, and get charged for the property damage resulting from the fact that b) the entire universe would be destroyed.

Since light-speed—about 1.08 *billion* km/h in driving units—is the cosmic speed limit, our universe is littered with weird laws of physics that safeguard anything from breaking it. The cosmos is gladly willing to flush common sense down the drain if it means protecting the sacred speed of light; both space and time bend to its whim. Space squeezes shorter, time creeps slower, and even matter itself gets heavier as you approach that limit.

If you jumped on a bike and pumped the pedals till you were rolling at 99% of the speed of light, you'd be 7.1 times shorter, time would pass 7.1 times slower, and you'd weigh about as much as a small car. Repeat this stunt in a car, and you'd weigh as much as a bus. Repeat it in a bus, and you'd definitely lose your bus licence.

The cosmos distorts itself in weirder ways as you tiptoe closer to the cosmic speed limit; if you *actually* had the audacity and magical ability to hit light-speed, those distortions would all become infinite, basically freezing time and causing space to collapse, as well as turning you into an infinitely-massive wrecking ball, obliterating the entire universe.

Of course, such a maddening thing couldn't happen in real-life.

Except that it often did. Our whole existence depended on it.

It takes a kick of 40,000 kilometres per hour to escape Earth's gravitational pull. You can imagine space like an ocean, and Earth like a riptide flowing downward at 40,000 km/h. If you want to fight against the current, you'll need to push forward faster than it's flowing backward.

For a brawny planet like Jupiter, you'll need to launch against the gravitational riptide at 215,000 km/h to escape. The Sun requires a blast of 2.16 *million* km/h to escape its gravitational riptide. If you crush a crapload of matter into a dense ball, its riptide of gravity pulls ever more, requiring even more speed to escape.

At some point, gravity gets so intense that your escape speed needs to be *more* than 1.08 billion km/h—the speed limit of the universe. At that point, *nothing* can escape, not even light itself, and the universe officially gives up on the whole idea of battling gravity, collapsing space into a black hole in an instant. That's all a black hole is, truth be told: just a small pocket of space being dragged downward faster than light.

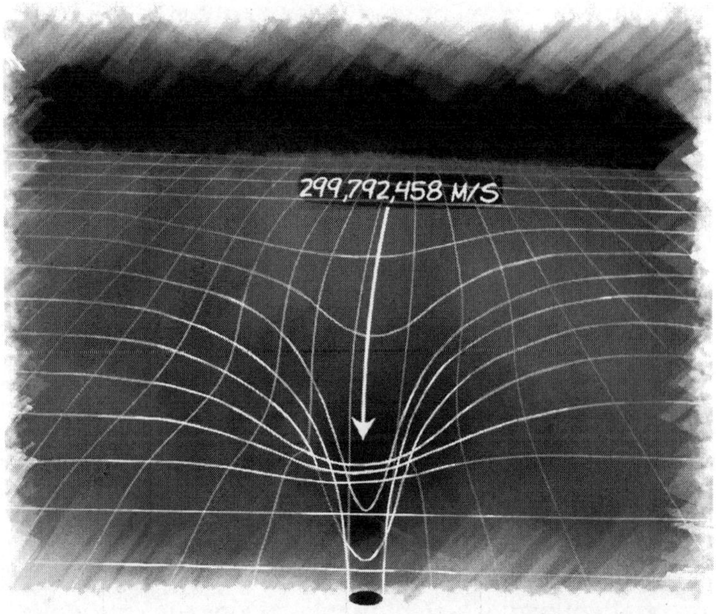

Of course, a "small pocket" is pretty ambiguous in astronomy; for black holes, this can mean anything from the size of New York City to 30 times wider than the solar system. It's on the bigger end of that spectrum where we find the seeds that sowed our galaxies.

Beyond the hellish pubescent years of cosmic inflation, our universe was still a bit of an early bloomer. In 2024, the James Webb Space Telescope snapped a photo of *JADES-GS-z14-0*, a galaxy that appeared just 290 million years after the Big Bang. We eventually realized that these immaculate early-bird galaxies are actually pretty common.

And black holes—the grim reapers of space—had somehow already ballooned to billions of times the mass of the Sun in less than a billion years, which makes about as much sense as a pumpkin growing from a seed to a planet-sized menace practically overnight. So what propelled such a speedy cosmic adolescence?

Matter of fact, it was dark matter that orchestrated this galactic assembly. Its gravitational pull guided the whole fiasco. But black holes finished it.

Most stars in the young universe were not too much bigger than the Sun, but a handful of them grew ridiculously big—big enough to eventually collapse into the largest black holes ever to gracefully suck on this universe. In 2011, a Cambridge study suggested that some of these first stars might have bloated to such mind-boggling sizes that their gravity dragged billions of baby stars into orbit around them, locked in by galaxy-sized globs of dark matter.

About two galactic birthdays, or 550 million Earth years, after the Big Bang, those dark globs could've ignited super-sized stars, up to 10 million times larger than the Sun, crushing their cores so hellishly dense that they collapsed into black holes immediately. These weren't your ordinary, supermarket-value black holes with a few times the mass of our Sun. These were millions of times heavier.

Much like a person being leeched upon by an indestructible cosmic mosquito, stars don't survive very long with black holes feeding inside them. In an act of celestial cannibalism, these stars were consumed from the inside-out, leaving behind the voided husk of supermassive black holes. With some help from dark matter, they became the centrepieces of swirling whirlpools of stars—and the galaxies were born.

Our own beloved Milky Way came together around 800 million years after the Big Bang, swirling up from a maelstrom of stars and dark matter. Since its formation, it's had about 58 galactic birthdays, making it a typical middle-aged galaxy. It would qualify for senior discounts in a galactic shopping mall.

Around 10 billion years ago, our Milky Way was greeted with a head-on splash from another galaxy known as the *Gaia Sausage*. It owes that delectable name to the space-based *Gaia* observatory, which plotted the orbits of millions of stars residing in our own galaxy that appeared to trace the vague shape of a sausage.

Turns out this sausage had intergalactic origins.

Like a cosmic burger arcing in an elegant billion-year-long flip, the Sausage sloshed right through our galaxy and delivered over 10 billion Suns' worth of stars and galactic gas. Its clouds rammed straight into the clouds of our Milky Way galaxy, setting off a fireworks extravaganza of millions of new stars that showered us with new heavy metals and other elements.

By a crude estimate, about 1-in-100 of our modern Milky Way's stars are native residents of the Gaia Sausage galaxy, and as those stars exploded and mingled with local stars, their dust got scattered across the Milky Way. That means, with some lengthy odds, the rocks and grit of Earth might've been made of atoms delivered from another galaxy. In a sense, our planet might have been cooked from the heavy metals of stars that migrated billions of light-years through space to land right on our cosmic doorstep.

All of this was thanks to the star-tossing roulette caused by black holes; their pull dragged billions of stars together, setting a perfect mixture for planets, watery chemistry, and eventually life. We're all too familiar with black holes being dubbed as ghastly cosmic menaces—and to our credit, they'd sooner rip our planet apart than provide us any pleasant shelter. But there's an eerie beauty about black holes too, especially thanks to the unbelievable way they knit the fabric of space and time.

What happens in a black hole, it seems, *stays* in a black hole, and our speculations about their innards are basically limited to the chalkboards of highly caffeinated physicists. But we've got *some* clues about what happens *before* you wholly fall into the hole.

The closer you're dragged to a black hole, the faster you move. As the relentless riptide of space shovels you down toward the speed of light, time ticks slower until it literally creeps to a standstill. At the edge of the black hole itself, as you hit light-speed, time freezes and locks you in place forever—at least to anyone watching it happen.

From our perspective, anything that's *ever* had the misfortune of stumbling down a black hole is *still* falling in, growing ever fainter, but still hovering there, frozen in time just above the blackened edge of the boundary. Black holes are the ultimate taxidermy, holding perfect relics in a timeless zone of space—relics as old as the universe itself, forever out of our reach.

The Star of the Show

Like most things in the universe, our solar system began with a bang.

The black hole at the core of our Milky Way, *Sagittarius A**, swirled our galaxy into its iconic spiral shape, sprinkling it with newborn stars. Somewhere around 20 galactic birthdays ago, about 4.6 billion years before the first human eyes glimpsed starlight, one desolate cloudy nebula collapsed under its gravity, clumping up a newborn star at its core. That star was our Sun, and whatever event triggered the nebula's collapse, we ought to be pretty thankful for it.

That exact event was suggested by astronomer Myriam Telus and colleagues in a 2012 paper, which found evidence that around 4.6 billion years ago, a star went supernova, blasting a high-pressure shockwave into deep space. That shockwave then rammed into a cloudy nebula—which just so happened to be ours—pushing on its dust with just enough force to collapse it, birthing the Sun and its planets. In that sense, we owe the existence of our solar system to the catastrophic obliteration of another one.

How could scientists possibly pinpoint such a long-lost explosion? Being blasted with a supernova shockwave is a lot like getting splashed with a bucket of paint: it leaves a massive stain behind. In cosmic terms, the stain is

* The asterisk is part of the black hole's name, pronounced "Sagittarius A-star."

Iron-60, a radioactive metal isotope that is the hallmark of a supernova—and the oldest rocks in our solar system are peppered with it, like stale icing on an obsidian cake that's 4.6 billion years past its expiration date.

Once our Sun blew up as the centerpiece of the collapsed nebula, the relentless force of its intense radiation booted most of that nebula back into the galaxy, leaving only a sparse cloud of dust behind. That dust became us.

Over about 100,000 years, heavier elements like nickel, silicon, and iron lumped up into hundreds of rocky planets across the solar system, setting the stage for a serious session of planet roulette. It was too hot near the Sun for gases like hydrogen and helium to get scooped up by the planets, in the same way snowballs don't roll too well in a steaming puddle.

In our solar system, a border known as the *frost line* appeared. It's a region around 700 million kilometres from the Sun where water turns to ice and, about 4.6 billion years ago, light fluffy gases first coalesced and clumped together into huge ballooning spheres—the spheres we now call the gas giants.

That frost line, not by coincidence, is between the orbits of Mars and Jupiter, forming the distinct boundary between the rocky planets and the gas giants. In the same way that light oil separates and floats on top of water when you mix them, the light gases of hydrogen and helium floated up to the outer brim of our solar system, leaving the heavier metals to sink down near the Sun's heated embrace.

When our solar system was forming, its most popular sport was planetary pinball. Call it what you will: bumper stars, ten-planet bowling, major-league spaceball—the Earth was born in the largest collision derby in the history of our star system. Less than one percent of all asteroids from this era actually survived to today.

Our planet formed along with about a hundred other rocky worlds and protoplanets, all sharing an intimate orbit. Rocks and dust were swept up by these rocky worlds like cosmic mops, and so the planets began to grow. Earth started off as a scrawny ball of rock around 30 kilometres wide—just a little larger than New York City—and snowballed its way into the massive sphere it is today. The Earth flung itself together 4.6 billion years in the past—about 19 galactic birthdays ago. On our galactic timescale, we've barely reached legal drinking age.

Around 4.45 billion years ago, in a deadly round of planetary pinball, Earth was dealt a serious smack by a Mars-sized protoplanet called Theia. Both worlds were obliterated, and even as our pulverized Earth hoisted itself back together, a massive chunk of debris stayed in orbit, settling under its gravity to become the Moon.

When it first appeared, the Moon orbited about 17 times closer to us and decorated our landscapes with over 200 times more moonlight. This would have made moonlit date nights just slightly more romantic in spite of the molten lava and endless meteorite impacts.

Adolescence is never an easy experience, and Earth had its fair share of teenage misery too. About 18 galactic years ago, our solar system entered an era known as the Late Heavy Bombardment, hammering each planet with a hailstorm of asteroids.

This meteor shower extraordinaire was likely caused by the gas giants Jupiter and Saturn, which slowly drifted outward in their orbits and eventually plowed into the minefield of leftover rocks from our solar system's earlier days. Thanks to the immense gravity of those two behemoth planets, rocks flew rampant in all directions.

But we might owe our existence to that too.

Chondrites, a special kind of asteroid, might have delivered every teaspoon of water on our planet, stored away in cosmic ice. In 2020, researchers at the Université de Lorraine ran simulations that showed chondrites could've dumped over three times more liquid water onto our fledgeling planet Earth than all the water in our modern oceans combined.

Perhaps the Earth's molten crust already held enough pent-up water to quench its own oceans without any help from meteors—or perhaps every glass we drink from our faucet was asteroid-delivered. That ancient water is literally everywhere; it's 60% of your body, filling your brain, flowing through your veins, and falling from the clouds. Our atoms came from the cores of stars, stirred up in a stew that might've come from distant asteroids.

To this day, the origin of the oceans remains a hotly and wetly debated subject.

When Earth's forecast finally dipped below 100°C, which happened about 17 galactic birthdays ago—3.9 billion Earth years back—an entire ocean's worth of rain condensed from hot steam in the skies and splattered down upon our planet's blackened surface. Over several million years, more than 1.3 billion cubic kilometres of water plummeted from the clouds in the most torrential downpour in our planet's history. If Noah thought he needed to build an ark for the flood written in *Genesis*, he definitely would have needed a fleet of cargo ships for this one.

Once the Earth's oceans had drizzled to the surface, the Moon began pulling our tides, which stabilized our planet's axis and regulated the seasons. It also gradually tugged on our planet's surface, slowing its rotation down from a speedy ten-hour-long spin to the 24-hour cycle we enjoy now. At last, we were able to call it a day.

Earth Gets a Life

If you took one glance at the Earth as it looked 3.8 billion years ago, you probably wouldn't have bet much on life taking hold there. The oceans marinated at a steamy 85°C as their sweltering waves crashed on lava-licked shores. Our planet popped so many volcanic pimples in its adolescence that its atmosphere became smothered in a hellish haze of methane, nitrogen, and carbon dioxide. Not a single breath of oxygen filled the air.

And that's exactly the environment in which life first evolved.

Similar to the mystique that surrounds the Big Bang, the scientific community still hasn't settled on a single theory for the origin of life. But following the latest evidence and the picture it paints, our planet began to show the symptoms of life's infection around 16 galactic birthdays ago—3.8 billion Earth years before today.

Perhaps life began in the basement of the oceans, where Earth's molten mantle gurgled hot plumes of minerals up through hydrothermal vents, billowing smoke into the water at around 400°C, and causing fantastic chemistry to stir. Perhaps it began in moist clay stews bubbling in ponds on the surface. Whatever began it, the atoms that had mingled in the hearts of distant stars were patched together into the molecules that would one day become part of you and me.

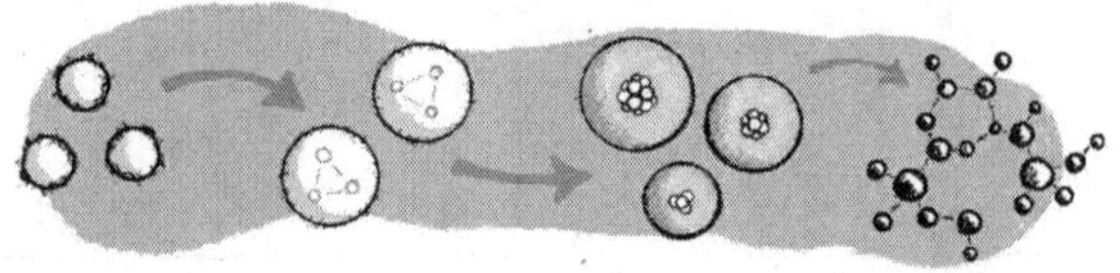

If there were a universal cookbook, life on Earth would be a salad, dressed in water and tossed in a blast furnace. The ingredients list is still growing—we're nowhere close to knowing it all—but the recipe's base would likely be some molecular mix of *nucleotides*, *amino acids*, and *fatty acids*. The first gave life a genetic code, the second gave it snippety tools to utilize, and the third wrapped it all in a protective shell. Toss quintillions of these molecules in an ocean-sized mixing bowl, sauté the salad at a high temperature, let it simmer for four billion years, and you shouldn't be surprised to find fish swimming in it.

Our recipe likely started with nucleotides—the tiny molecules that make up the rungs on the double-stranded twisted ladder of DNA. If our genetic code were a book, nucleotides would be its letters, and cells would be its readers. At the peak of Earth's asteroid hailstorm, four letters—tagged as G, U, A, and C—were delivered en masse into the oceans.

Nucleotides each have small packets of atoms on their tip, like a pencil eraser, holding a sugar molecule and a phosphate molecule—and those two simply *love* clinging together. In one of many theories for life's origin, these nucleotides chained up end-to-end like an atomic conga line, stacking into RNA molecules—the first strands of genetic code. These were the blueprints that kicked off a four-billion-year-long chemical reaction that eventually gave rise to even vastly more complex copying machines, such as yourself.

These lifeless snippets of RNA might seem unimpressive, but so does a twisted-up elastic band sitting on a tabletop—and as we know, even those elastics are capable of springing to life in unexpected ways with a little pent-up energy.

In 1982, the *Self-Splicing Intron* was discovered—a small RNA strand that was capable of chopping itself in half. Pretty impressive for a lifeless clump of atoms. Even more impressive, the *R3C Ligase Ribozyme* was whisked up in a lab in 2002, and it was able to assemble its own nucleotide letters, bond with them, and construct a clone of itself.

Imagine finding a Lego model that built its own Lego bricks.

We haven't yet stumbled upon a natural Lego-building Lego set, but our best evidence for those self-slicing RNA strands is their direct descendants; they're still alive today.

Even as life charioted forward into vastly more complex critters, those self-slicing strings were so successful that they're still here. Some plants like tuber potatoes and tomatoes are often ambushed by pests called *viroids*—little loops of RNA that are so laughably simple, they're mistaken for bits and pieces of the plant's own genetics. Viroids are the last living relics of solo-surviving molecules. Everything since then has been founded on teamwork.

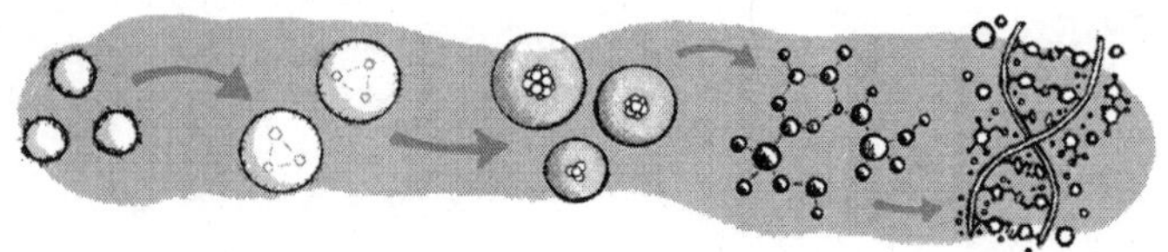

There's a living fossil in every one of your cells—an ancient relic of cooperation that goes back almost four billion years. While RNA strands could probably copy themselves from the beginning, they were awfully fragile, often smashed to pieces by slight temperature changes in the water—and besides, life was essentially limited in complexity to a ramen noodle soup of genetic spaghetti strands. Our jump from dead chemistry to living cells was orchestrated by the second ingredient in our recipe for life: amino acids.

Just like nucleotides, amino acids chained up like magnets, clinging together into conga-line rows known as proteins—yes, ordinary proteins. All the slices of cheese, blocks of tofu, and protein bars you've ever consumed were, in essence, highly-developed lumps of amino acids scavenged up from the Earth's formation.

This is where those letters of G, U, A, and C finally come in. Amino acids are fervently attracted to those letters, but each acid favours a specific combo. Line up the nucleotide letters C·A·G, and you'll attract the amino acid Glutamine. The conga line A·C·C drags in the amino acid Threonine. You'll need G·U·G to bring

in Valine. With the right patterns, any combination is possible—although most of them are useless.

Across the oceans, this chemical matchmaking hub brewed at breakneck speed. Frenzies of proteins began to speckle the water.

Over time, more intricate proteins began emerging, and some began to fall into a sort of partnership with the RNA strands. In one case, an enzyme called the *polymerase* developed a knack for photocopying new RNA strands from an original copy. More molecular partnerships—an enzyme called the *nuclease* had a habit of slicing RNA in half like snippety atomic scissors, while the *ligase* evolved to tack two strands together like atomic glue.

Having these handiwork machines around was so much better than going solo that the blueprints of proteins were etched right into our genome, letter for letter. The protein of *insulin*, which lets sugars seep into our bodies, is etched in a string of 350 nucleotide letters in our cells.

About 1% of our entire human genetic code is just one long string of letters coding for various proteins to be constructed. It's like an oversized library that only offers self-help books—and the librarian is the only one who ever reads them.

In a way, our genetic code gave amino acids a method of copying themselves, while the amino acids gave us a toolkit of molecular machinery to accelerate the evolution of RNA and its DNA descendants. In a harrowing universe that's constantly trying to smash the delicate system of living things, it really pays to cooperate.

Eventually, we evolved a massive protein called the *ribosome*, which itself is a protein-building factory of awesome efficiency. It's the crowned pinnacle of teamwork between proteins and RNA, and it's so unbelievably ubiquitous that it's chuffing along in every organism on planet Earth right now, from the birds in trees to the trees themselves, from the bacteria in the rivers to the bacteria on your tongue. It ticks like clockwork inside all of your cells, brewing over a billion proteins every second.

Even with a genetic code and snippety machines to service it, life was about as functional as a roofless airplane before a protective hull evolved to enclose it all. This is where fatty acids—our final main ingredient—might have come in. In a pinch, they can assemble into microscopic bubbles known as membranes.

These acids are two-faced; their heads are incredibly attracted to water, while their atomic tails repel water with a fervent hatred. When water is present—and in the ocean, it's pretty damn hard to avoid—fatty acids are forced to flutter into an oily bubble-shaped globule to remain stable. While their heads float freely in the water's seductive allure, their tails are repulsed by water, and the only waterless haven they can find is the swarming company of other fatty acid tails. To avoid water, tails are naturally drawn together, and so, like an unrequited love triangle, tails stick with heads, heads attract water, and water absolutely revolts tails.

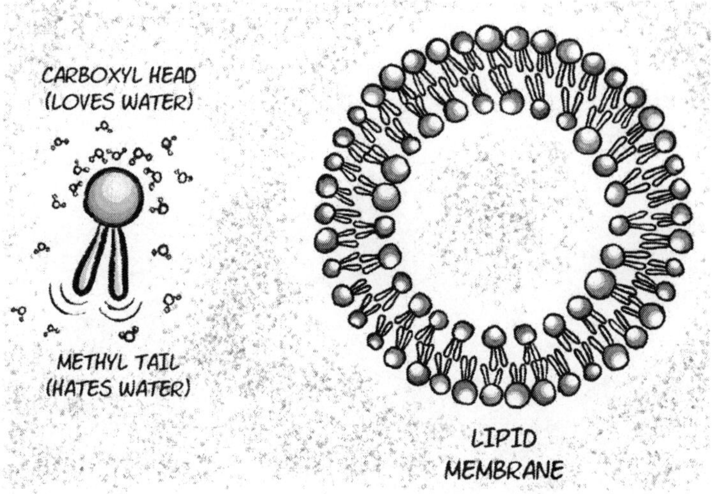

With these three ingredients brewing at full throttle, somewhere in the primal oceans of Earth, in the most profound event in the known universe, a small clump of refurbished stardust came alive. One small cell was born. Its name was Luca.

To be pedantic, its true name was the *Last Universal Common Ancestor*, but for purposes of endearment, its acronym is far sweeter. From that cell, an inordinate trillion-or-so generations later, we humans came to walk this planet. We all share a root back to single-celled

LUCA, every species in the world, unbroken across life's history. This was the seed that sprouted the enormous tree of life—and it's growing strong after 3.8 billion years and counting.

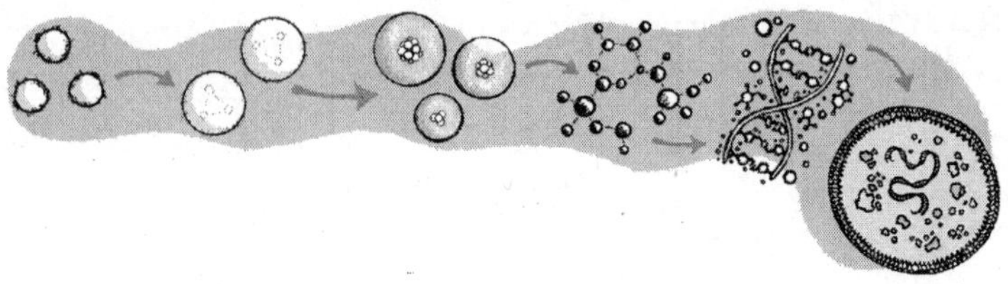

The Cosmic Lottery

Our species is a twig sprouting from a small branch at the edge of a colossal tree of life—a tree whose roots extend almost all the way back to our planet's formation. One trunk unifies them all at the base: our *Last Universal Common Ancestor*, the cell named LUCA.

If you look at life's evolution over its four-billion-year-long history on this planet, you'll notice that the genomes of creatures keep getting longer and longer. In other words, although the first cells began with simple strings of genetic code, they've gotten vastly more complex over the eons and epochs.

Life began like a sentence. It then expanded into a paragraph, then a chapter, and finally into the genetic encyclopedias we are nowadays. The first simple bacteria to swim our oceans functioned with just 50,000 nucleotide letters of DNA in their little cellular bodies.

By the time cells evolved a nucleus, this genome had expanded to 2.8 million letters. The cyanobacteria (we're about to meet them in the next chapter) boasted 14 million letters. The first sea sponges contained over 200 million letters, jellyfish stored about 275 million, and pufferfish were stocked with 400 million. Skip ahead to the dinosaurs, and our good friend *Tyrannosaurus rex* had a genome that was 1.8 billion letters long. One small asteroid and 65 million years later, humans have evolved a genome containing 3.1 billion nucleotide letters, tightly knit into your cells to produce the long and elegant genome that makes you the person you are.

This long and evolving genetic encyclopedia is always being revised and copied. If you've raised children, congratulations on being a copyeditor of the human genome.

But the genome of life isn't merely growing at random. In 2006, biologist Alexei Sharov boiled our entire evolution down to one single pattern: life's genome seems to be getting about 10 times longer every 1.1 billion years—an absurdly crude pattern, but one that's held up across four billion years of Earth's history.

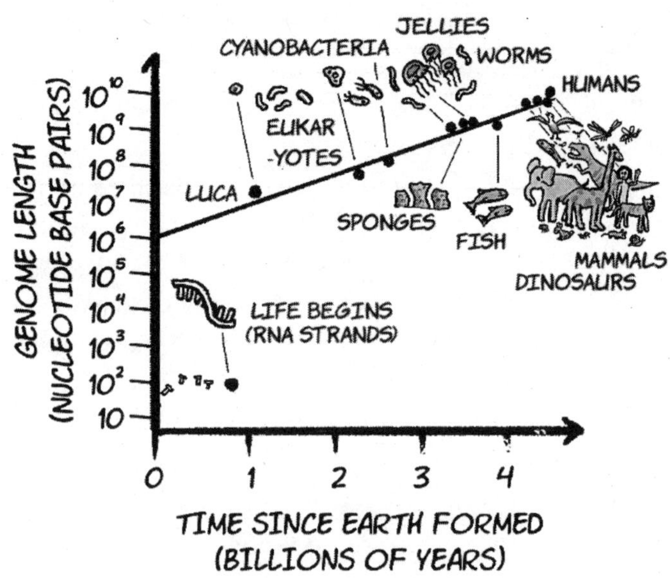

SHAROV. AA GENOME INCREASE AS A CLOCK FOR THE ORIGIN AND EVOLUTION OF LIFE. BIOL DIRECT 1 17 (2006) HTTPS://DOI.ORG/10.1186/1745-6150-1-17

If we follow Sharov's curve right back to the origin of life, it's pretty hard to ignore that dramatic and sudden leap right at the beginning. We know that life perhaps began with an unruly blend of self-slicing RNA strands that were, at best, around 200 nucleotide letters long. We also know that fully-formed cells were scooting around the oceans 3.8 billion years ago—and those already had 50,000 nucleotide letters.

In this hairpin window of time, just a few hundred million years, life somehow took this baffling jump from genetic spaghetti noodles to intricate cellular machines. It's like purchasing a Lego box and finding that the overpriced model you wanted to build had already self-assembled in the time it took you to drive home from the toy store. Not impossible, but remarkable.

If you're a fan of mainstream theories—and yes, most scientists are—this hairpin jump in our genome length was likely thanks to RNA being so fragile. Add some heat, a little radiation, a seasoning of acid, and those strands of RNA simply shattered like snowflakes. Mutations were so ridiculously common, and happened so often, RNA couldn't sit still for a second. Its evolution rocketed ahead at breakneck speed, eventually stumbling upon DNA—the double-stranded brand of RNA, which was more stable, grinding that speedy evolution to a halt.

Now, if you're a fan of fringe ideas—and willing to step outside the realm of science-fact, into the larger theatre of science-speculation, and take this all with a colossal grain of salt, Sharov proposed a second explanation for this sudden jump from RNA to proper cells. When he published his genome graph, he imagined this: if genomes have been growing 10-fold every 1.1 billion years, that pattern might work backwards too. He extended the trend back 10-12 *billion* years into the past—just enough to whittle life's genome down to a few hundred letters, which is about as long as those miniature RNA noodles which may have kickstarted life itself.

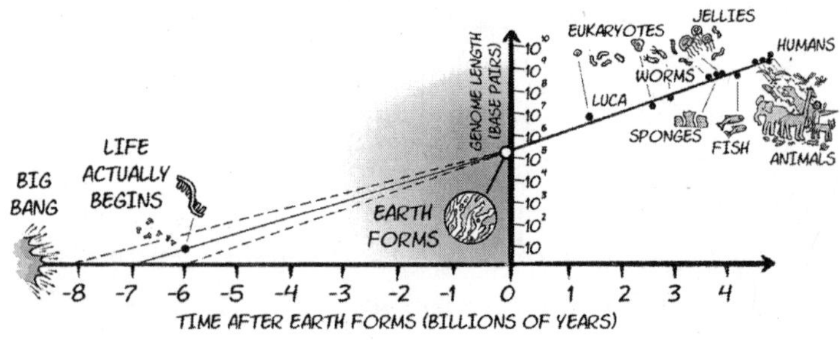

If the universe had a to-do checklist, the Earth wouldn't have even been an *idea* 12 billion years ago—but this graph begs the question: how long has life been brewing in our universe? Twelve billion years is more than enough to fill that awkward jump from basic molecules to fully-fledged cells; with billions of extra years to spare, life could've tinkered with those traits more gradually.

Unfortunately, Sharov's idea takes a century of studies in evolutionary biology and dropkicks them straight out the window. His extended graph was critiqued and mostly disproven in the last decade, but the idea—that life might've evolved across the universe before Earth ever snowballed itself into existence—is nothing new. It's known as *panspermia*, which is about as grotesque as it sounds: a kind of planetary crossbreeding.

Rocks are often tossed between planets in an asteroid-driven game of meteorite tennis. we've found bits and pieces of Mars on Earth, chunks of the Moon on Earth, and even a small slab of Earth on the Moon during the Apollo 14 mission. In all those samples, we've spied the raw ingredients of life.

Two separate spacecraft missions, *Hayabusa2* in 2020 and *OSIRIS-REx* in 2023, visited the asteroids Ryugu and Bennu respectively, scooping up samples and bringing back untouched relics of the most ancient rocks in the solar system. In that immaculate mix of stones, scientists found *uracil* and *adenine*—the nucleotide letters U and A—cooked into the rocks themselves. In the same way finding sugar and flour *doesn't* mean you've discovered cake, these two molecules alone aren't a hands-down discovery of life. But they bring us one step closer.

NASA's planet-spotting *Kepler* space telescope put in a conservative estimate that there's about 600 quintillion (6×10^{20}) Earth-like planets in our known universe. Even if life is a cosmic lottery, 600 quintillion tickets is plenty—and asteroids might spread it far and wide.

We like to imagine a kind of "tree of life" on Earth that ends with modern humans and begins its roots with LUCA, our little cellular ancestor. But it's also possible that our entire tree is merely a sequel to life's *actual* origin story—some even vaster tree whose branches extend to distant worlds we've never laid our eyes upon. So if we ever contact extraterrestrial life, it might just be the grandest family reunion we've ever planned.

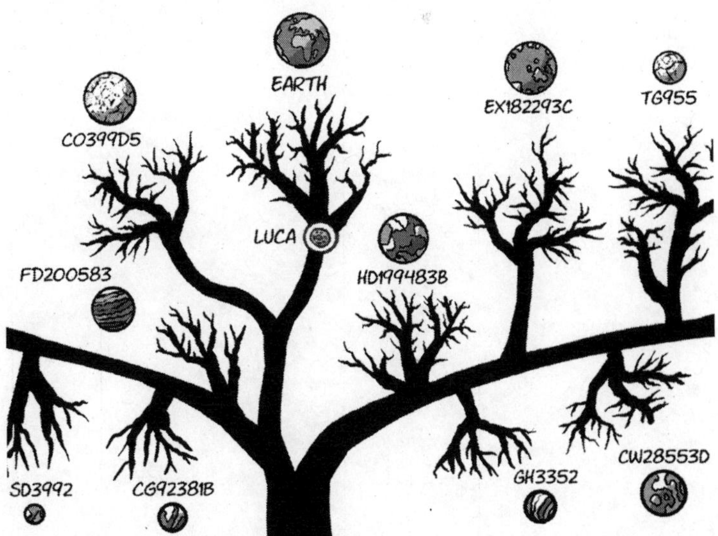

The Stardust Comes Alive

At face value, how could humans be the distant cousins of mosquitoes? How could fishflies be related to actual fish, and mayflies be related to mayflowers and mayapples and mayweed? How did a single cell evolvc into the mind-baffling spread of diverse life we've got today?

The secret lies in DNA and the fact that it is serviced by terrible photocopiers. Our best laser-jet printers can easily splat 100 million pixels onto a page without making a single error. If we downgraded those printers to the accuracy of DNA's printer—an enzyme known as the *DNA polymerase* which cranks along in cells—it would mess up about 1,000 of those pixels, slightly changing the original picture.

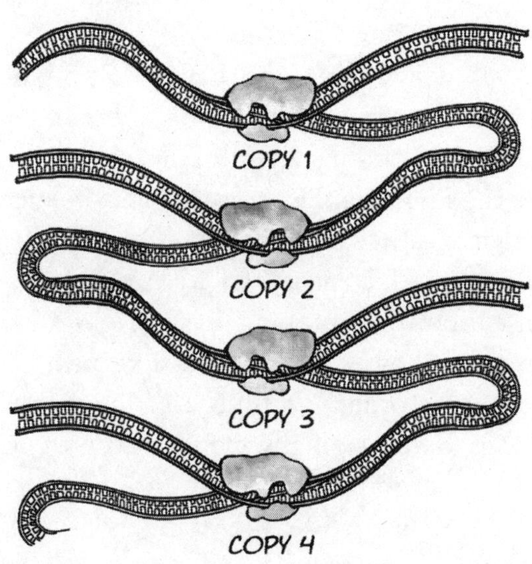

Since life is, at a basic level, just a photocopying machine that extrudes offspring instead of paper, this error-ladened printing process slowly edits the genetic code until it becomes an entirely separate species.

Sometimes these edits ruin everything, like *plant albinism*, a mutation that kills plants by robbing them of chlorophyll—their own green lifeblood. But sometimes the edit is fantastic, like the mutation that sculpted the first land-hobbling legs in our fish-descendant ancestors some 360 million years ago. Life is an aimless game of chance, and this world, the game's arena, is known to flip on a dime.

Our oldest cousins branched off around 3.5 billion years ago when bacteria and archaea began squirming in the oceans. These folks were all pretty simple and microscopic, but thanks to a mutual accident of their evolution, both evolved the exact same mode of transport: a thin waggling tail known as the flagellum.

In a world where energy is a token of survival, it didn't take long for bacteria to develop a habit of drinking sunlight—photosynthesis, the hallmark trait of plants. Ancient cyanobacteria were the first to use it, basking in the limitless light of our star, dumping oxygen into the air as a waste gas. Photosynthesis turned out to be such a lethal weapon that it came close to wiping this planet sterile of life itself—an odd fact, given that it's literally everywhere.

Despite how breathtaking life's origin was, taking a breath would have been impossible until a crucial event that blossomed around 2.4 billion years ago. Earth's skies were originally clouded in a thick mix of methane and carbon dioxide. It sounds horrific, but life called it home. Earth was the orange planet of life—a methane-stocked paradise.

But then, cyanobacteria came to rule. Their primary fuel engine, photosynthesis, began to mass-produce trillions of tons of oxygen. For a while, the oceans captured the excess supply; deep-sea iron metal managed to couple up with the oxygen, rusting to form iron-oxides. Those telltale bands of rust are still visible in the deepest crevices of the ocean.

But even rusted iron couldn't pack the full supply of fresh air. Soon, oxygen saturated the oceans and leaked into the atmosphere in a pollution frenzy called the *Great Oxygenation Event*, and over its 400-million-year span, our skies finally turned blue. The iconic "Blue Planet" only really became a thing 2.4 billion years ago, 11 galactic birthdays before today.

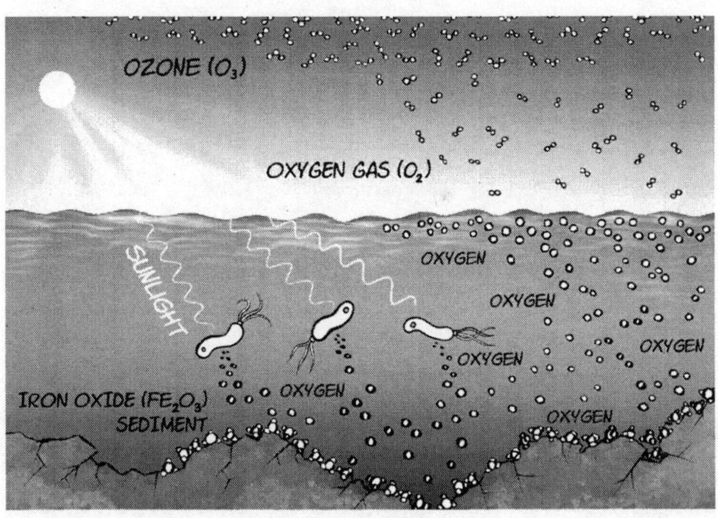

Oxygen was a sharp gas that life had never encountered before. Most life didn't breathe oxygen, so when our planet became shrouded with it, disaster ensued, wiping out nearly 90% of all living cells in a gassy massacre of extinction. The noxious fumes of oxygen nearly sniped out the very cyanobacteria that produced it.

Our climate went through a literal sea-change. Oxygen is worse than methane at sponging up the warmth of sunlight, so when our skies evicted methane in favour of oxygen, it dropped the world's temperature from its steamy 60-85°C to a more temperate 15°C, sending the environment into chaos. In the upper atmosphere, oxygen bonded in triplets to make ozone (O_3) which coated our entire planet in a layer of natural sunscreen.

Ozone is fantastic at absorbing the UV radiation emitted by the Sun, and when our ozone layer formed, it shielded the entire surface of Earth from 99% of that radiation—and since those rays are practical sniper bullets to our delicate DNA, Earth's new bullet-proof vest blanketed the bare, windswept continents, and set the stage for life to eventually hobble onto land.

And life itself, despite its near extinction, carried on and evolved in its new world. Life's a remarkable adapter—it evolved to breathe oxygen, and we are living proof of that adaptation. Every breath we take is filled with the sustenance belched from a trillion cyanobacteria living on a planet gone wild.

About 1.9 billion years down history lane, 1.9 billion Earth years ago, life went through another drastic shift. In an ancient act of cannibalism, one cell devoured another, but rather than digesting it alive, the eaten cell was stored as a pocket purse for our genetic code, which became the cell's nucleus. That nucleus sprouted an entire new branch on the tree of life, the *eukaryotes*, and we're on it. We evolved from that 1.9-billion-year root, and we're just one tendril among its 8.7 million branches of creatures.

But this wasn't the only incident of cell cannibalism—not even remotely close. Our entire existence hinges on cannibalism and the fact that, back then, it was a popular move.

Cyanobacteria, in their glorious rule of Earth, split into several new species. Among those were little green-tinted pods known as *chloroplasts*, and for 200 million years, they swam free, drinking sunlight and photosynthesizing it into energy. But an ancient act of cannibalism landed chloroplasts *inside* a larger cell—and rather than being eaten, chloroplasts struck a bond. With their photosynthesis, chloroplasts cooked sunlight into free energy for their host cell, and the host offered a safe residence for the chloroplasts. It was no Airbnb, but the rental remains to this day, tinting plants in their signature shade of green.

Mitochondria, the infamous powerhouses of the cell, were *also* free-swimming bacteria until they too got captured and employed 1.45 billion years ago. Since that fateful day, our cells have profiteered on their energy.

Mitochondria kept their own DNA; they're *still* dividing and multiplying *inside* your cells and body. But they're not free-living anymore, and for their long term survival, it was worth it. They can't live without us, and we can't survive without them. Remove a mitochondrion from its host cell, and the cell dies from sugar starvation. That's perhaps the first case of domestication in the world.

But the single-celled species of *dinoflagellates* took the notion of cannibalism to a whole new level. Ever since their evolution about 1.5 billion years ago, they've been profiteering on the profiteering of other profiteer cells. Many dinoflagellates contain smaller cells known as diatoms—a species of algae with a distinct, red-tinted hue—and *those* diatoms contain even smaller red alga cells consumed by *them* about 1.2 billion years ago, like a microscopic Matryoshka Doll. Employment is as old as life itself; if you can't sell it, cell it.

This kind of partnership evolved over 25 different times across the board, from plant and animal cells to fungi and protists. Molecules teamed up to work as cells, and much later, cells teamed up to work in colonies.

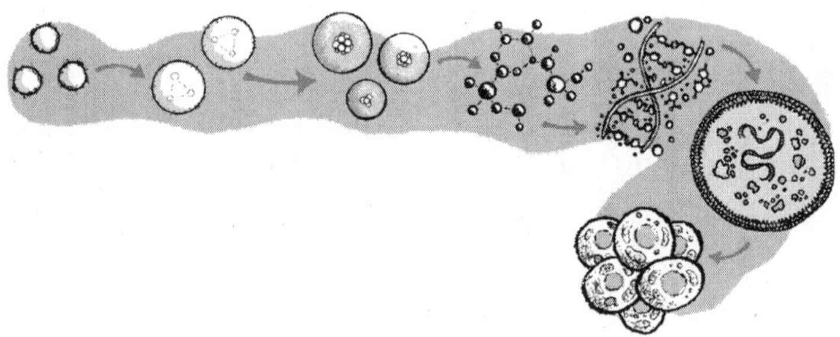

An Ode to the Viruses

When life forked into its three enormous domains—the bacteria, the archaea, and eukaryotes—a fourth group lingered backstage. They never quite became alive, but they're hardly dead either. These cantankerous critters, the viruses, have been training their weapons on our cells for almost four billion years, but despite them being our sworn enemies, viruses might deserve a smidge of our respect.

When you unravel the entire human genome, you'll find that a staggering *eight percent* of it can be traced right back to our seasonal suckers. Viruses might be lifeless sacks of protein, but within them lies the loose weave of their RNA/DNA genetic code. When viruses besiege a cell, in addition to hijacking it into a vicious virus-making machine, they sometimes leave behind a small trace of their genetic code.

Make no mistake; most viruses don't care much for leaving genetic tidbits behind. Our dear friend COVID-19, for example, is ruthless enough to take a direct strike at the nucleus of a cell, tossing its deceptive RNA into a swarming nest of cut-and-paste molecules known as *RNA polymerases*. In mere hours, the naïve cell mistakes COVID's genome for its own, believing that it contains the genetic code for an important protein. That protein is actually a locked-and-loaded COVID-19 virus shell, and once the godforsaken cell realizes what it's building, the virus army has already destroyed it.

But another kind, known as *retroviruses*, are more devious. They stitch their own genetic code right into the DNA of their victim cell, quite literally becoming a part of the very instruction manual our cells read to survive. In some devastating cases like HIV, this implant soon erupts into a ferocious swarm of viruses, destroying the cell. But over a hundred known viruses employ this tactic, and most are harmless. In most cases, viruses leave their implants in our genomes, and it just remains there.

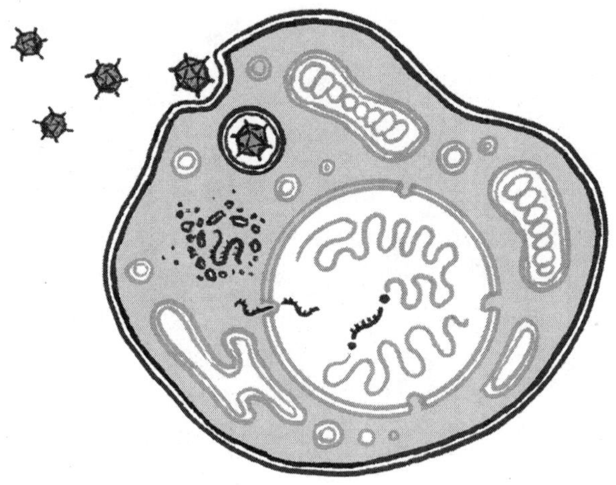

So across billions of years, viruses served as a kind of FedEx postal service for genetic codes, scooting around the oceans and skies, transmitting genes to and fro in their microscopic delivery packets. We wouldn't be nearly as advanced if it weren't for viruses.

The ability to have babies, for obvious reasons, is the only mechanism keeping the entire animal kingdom alive and well. Most bacteria, protists and archaea avoided the inconvenience of sex by keeping their self-splitting habit. But if you're like most animals, plants, or fungi, chances are cloning yourself is not an option, leaving babies as the one-stop-shop reproductive solution.

But how do you seize the means of reproduction?

Manufacturing a child requires two gametes—two semi-loaded cells, each holding one half of the full baby's genetic code. In animals, at least, those gametes are the egg and the sperm. To fuse those half-genetic codes, the two gametes need to burrow into each other.

Here's where viruses likely come in. Cell membranes, like the hull encasing an airplane, are pretty much evolved *not* to break, so the notion of *burrowing* inside cells is almost impossible without a protein known as HAP2, serving as a lock that fuses two cell membranes together like droplets.

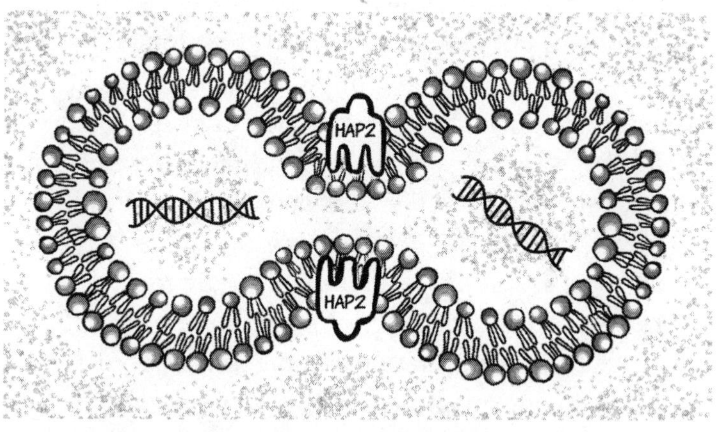

That lock is so ancient in life's history that insects, worms, corals, sea sponges, jellyfish, and algae contain it. But viruses predate them all, and a Cornell study from 2017 found that we might owe our entire reproductive life to a couple of ancient viruses snooping the HAP2 protein into our genome. If you were once born, which seems likely, give kudos to viruses for that.

As biologist Michael Slezak pointed out, if that lock hadn't evolved, life probably wouldn't have evolved much beyond sea sponges.

The fact that you're still reading this is hinting at the sheer quality of the *myelin fibres* in your brain—a material that coats nerve cells and boosts their electrical efficiency by 15-30 times. We didn't evolve it ourselves; a 2024 Cambridge study found its probable origin, in a retrovirus carrying *RetroMyelin* in its hull—yet another snooping incident.

Myelin was a crucial step in evolving the brains of mammals and fish. If we toss away myelin, we literally lose our minds and nerve; we suffer from multiple sclerosis. So if you've had a thought today, which seems likely, kudos to viruses again.

Viruses might've even delivered the protein *syncytin* into our genome about 200 million years ago. It's the very protein that allows the cells of a growing baby to affix to the wall of the womb, eventually growing into the placenta and the umbilical cord that kept you alive for nine months before your birthday. If you developed inside a womb, which again seems likely, kudos once again to viruses.

As someone who's had a bout with COVID-19, I'll admit that viruses aren't pleasant. But after four billion years of genetic mishmashing, they might deserve an inkling of our gratitude.

The Explosion of the Cambrian

Our planet, far beyond its flaming adolescence, still had a habit of dressing in goth. The evidence suggests that about 710 million years back in time—about three galactic years before yesterday—our planet was decked in a chic coating of white glaciers.

Today, we are caught in the onslaught of global warming, but back then, our planet was in a global cooling crisis. In 1969, Soviet climatologist Mikhail Budyko imagined the scenario that if our planet's polar ice caps ever expanded to cover over one-third of its surface, Earth would be plunged into a runaway deep-freeze—and that's exactly what happened.

Ice shines piercingly bright against the darkness of space, reflecting about 90% of the sunlight hitting it. That's great for keeping Earth cool, but coolness has a limit. With enough icing on the globe, our planet loses its sunlight-soaking abilities, making Earth cooler, triggering yet more ice, reflecting more heat, cooling more, icing more, and so on. It's a feedback loop.

That ice-crisis is precisely what planetary scientist Francis Macdonald uncovered in 2010 when he found fossil evidence of glaciers candidly chilling at our planet's equator back in the *Cryogenian* period. Some 700 million years ago, our planet fell to the biting temperature of 5°C and was lumped into a worldwide snowball, perhaps even twice.

But our planet came out of its permafrost goth era some 635 million years back, and temperatures began to rise, oxygen filled the sky again, and life erupted in the biggest biological rollercoaster ride in history, the Cambrian Explosion.

This rollercoaster ride launched about 540 million years ago—around 2.4 galactic birthdays back in our timeline—and it rocked the whole world. For the first time, cells not only teamed up in colonies, but those colonies teamed up as organs. Entire factions of cells emerged, each with a unique role in keeping their organism alive.

As cells started living together, their lifestyles and habits shifted to accommodate their new roomies. All cells are born with their organism's full genetic code—a complete instruction manual on how to run any survival task. But in full colonies, cells didn't need to be crafty know-it-all survivalists anymore. It was more efficient to divvy up tasks and specialize in just one.

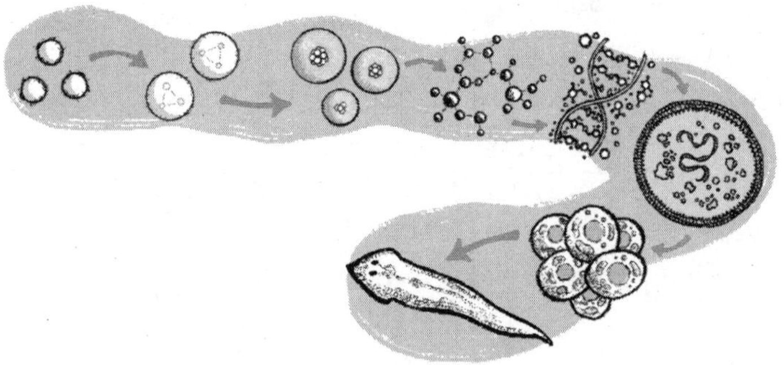

Of course, cells didn't really *know* what tasks to take on; this kind of specialization began thanks to a common trait shared between cells and teenagers: both will snap under peer pressure like toothpicks under a hydraulic press.

To get cells to conform, all it takes is a certain chemical. Take a newborn cell, immerse it with a protein called C-EBP, and it'll immediately shut down all its genes *except* for the skin-cell-related ones, and voilà, you've got a skin cell. Spray it down with another chemical called TGF-β, and it'll shut down all but the muscle-cell-related genes, becoming a myocyte—a muscle cell. Give it GM-CSF, and it'll become a white blood cell. It's truly just cellular peer pressure. If neighbouring cells are doing it, they'll emit chemicals that push nearby cells to follow suit.

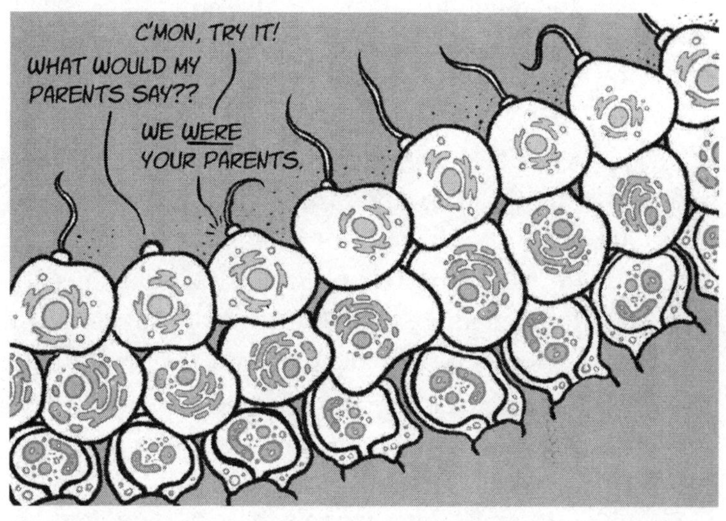

Sight-seeing was one of the first jobs cells embraced. From ancient trilobites to flatworms to fish and octopi and mammals, sight was so quintessential for survival that eyes popped up 65 separate times in life's evolution, with no link between them. On a brightly-lit planet like Earth, eyes evolved in almost every crevice of complex life—a natural checkpoint of life's evolution. Perhaps it's a checkpoint for life everywhere in our universe.

With cells honing in their skills, life gained a huge swath of abilities. It could see, touch, and listen. But to eclipse it all, life could *think* about things.

Because you're reading these words, it's obvious that brains evolved at least once. But thanks to a handful of fossils from the Cambrian, it's now becoming apparent that the brain might have evolved *two* separate times, yet another jackpot of nature.

The nervous system, complete with all its touchy neurons, felt its way into our history around 570 million years ago. But pinpointing *which* ancestor first grew a brain has proven difficult, since until lately, biologists were torn between two answers. It was down to sea sponges versus comb jellies.

If you trace our genetic family tree back 600 million years, all animals share one nimble ancestor known as the *urchoanozoan*—a mouthful in its name, but not in its size, spanning less than a millimetre long. Before its long-lost descendants evolved into modern animals, two distant species forked away from us to begin their own lineages.

On the one branch, *Ctenophora*—the comb jellies.

On the other, *Porifera*—the sea sponges.

Comb jellies these days have a simple nervous system and a pulpous brain that undulates their tentacles back and forth, wafting them through the water. Sea sponges haven't got any of that mental gadgetry. They're sponges, after all.

If you had to guess which of these creatures split off from our ancestors sooner, you'd be justified to choose the more primitive one—the sea sponges—because it makes sense that a more basic creature would evolve earlier, with the brain only arriving later.

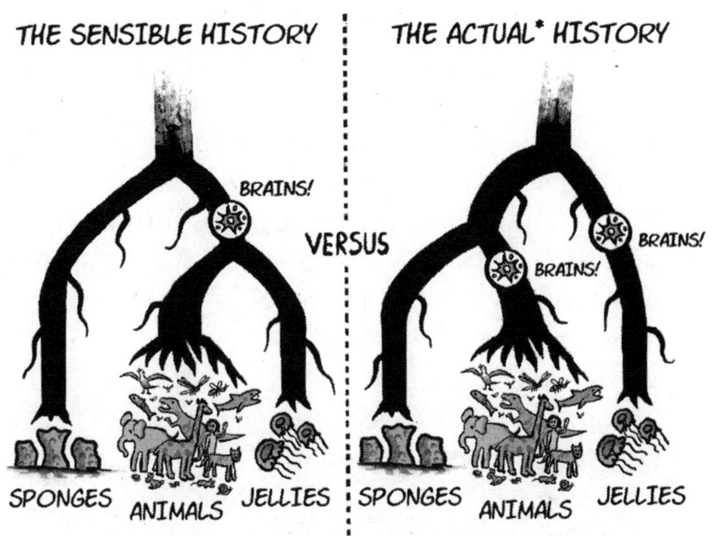

But in 2023, biologist Darrin Schultz and colleagues mapped the genome of comb jellies to reach a new hypothesis—the stark idea that sea sponges actually came *second* in our history.

In their findings, brainy comb jellies probably branched off *first* around 700 million years ago; brainless sea sponges branched off second 100 million years later; and 30 million years after that, the first brains began popping up in our animal ancestors.

This paints a bizarre history. Either sea sponges gradually lost their minds over millions of years, or *whole brains* literally evolved twice—once in our branch of modern animals, and again in the long-separated lineage of the comb jellies. That's about as whack as your girlfriend inheriting *your* family heirloom from *her* family.

The neurons in comb jellies look alien compared to ours. In a 2023 paper, Astrid Medhus and colleagues found that comb jellies' brains have no synapses—no long tendrils weaving between the cells to transmit electric signals. Instead, it's all jumbled up into a single gelatinous blob. It seems that brains, however diverse, might be a natural checkpoint of evolution too.

On dry land, plants and fungi were storming into the soil. Even though mushrooms and green plants look so similar, those two families couldn't have less in common. We and plants got separated about a billion years ago, while fungi clung onto our family tree about 35 million years longer. And a lot can happen in 35 million years.

Thanks to that extended family time, by the time fungi finally separated from us animals and started sprouting up on rocky land around 480 million years ago, they were closer-related to modern *humans* than any living plants.

And it makes sense—most plants self-serve their own food from sunlight. Animals and fungi both share the need to devour other species to get their nutrients. We both dissolve our food with digestive enzymes; fungi squeeze them into the soil and leech the nutrients from there; we animals have a stomach for the exact same job.

We've still got 50% of our genes in common.

On land, a wedded partnership between plants and fungi began to evolve another kind of brain. As plants sprouted roots deeper into the soil, fungi followed suit and extended their own spindled root net known as the *mycelium*. Those roots began to mingle, forming a planet-crossing web—over 390 million years before the internet ever graced this world.

THE WOOD-WIDE WEB

Mushroom caps, which you might stumble upon in the forest—sometimes literally—are just the sprouting tips of the vast mycelial network. Nutrients and water flow through it, plus a fringe of electric signals that have even evolved a very primitive version of short-term memory.

In a 2019 Cardiff study, biologist Melanie Savoury and her colleagues grew a miniature mycelium, which fully navigated to its food source, and then, in a brand-new bed of soil, recalled its pathway with 75% accuracy. The mycelial network sends its signals at a painstakingly slow pace of four millimetres per hour—about eight quadrillion times slower than internet—but the message gets across.

The mycelial network, nicknamed the *wood-wide web*, is engrained into the planet itself. Underneath your feet, one handful of forest soil contains over 2,000 kilometres of mycelial tubes intricately woven into the dirt. With them, plants began to sprout, and our formerly stone-grey barren landscape got a green makeover. It was here that Earth first began to look remotely Earth-like, 460 million years ago—two galactic birthdays before now.

As a crude estimate, across all four billion hectares of forestry on Earth's surface, a grand total of five million light-years of mycelium are girdling in nooks and crannies across the world. If we unspooled that into one strand, we could lasso the Andromeda galaxy, loop back around to the Milky Way, and then some.

As cells worked together in tight-knit creatures, they began to face new threats. Life still faced the age-old pestering of viruses, but now that it lived in billion-cell tribes, each individual cell was ill-equipped to fight alone.

And so, about 500 million years ago, a new role began to specialize: the immune system. Its main purpose was to devour intruders, a kind of internal army that scouted the body and, with the sculpting touch of a half-billion years of evolution, enlisted a slew of cells to fight.

Neutrophil cells evolved a knack for blasting toxins and inflammation. Plasma cells learned to build Y-shaped proteins known as antibodies to flag their enemies. The notorious *Natural Killer* cells sought nothing more than to obliterate any infected body cells—its *own* body cells—to thwart the infection as a sacrifice for the greater good. About two billion of those sacrificial cells are slain inside your body *every day* for your own self-defence.

The immune system, in its eons-long struggle against viruses and bacteria, battle-hardened itself into a lethal mechanism. The rallying cries of the immune system are chemicals known as *cytokines*—a batch of proteins primed to set off inflammation and launch the offensive strike of nearly two trillion armed cells.

With life weaponized, it grew quicker than ever.

Back in the oceans, life began to collaborate. Just like our single-celled ancestors teamed up with chloroplasts and mitochondria to strike a cellular alliance, clownfish and sea anemones started to depend on each other. So did gobies and pistol shrimp, sharks and pilot fish, each owing a debt to the other. Coral reefs sprang up across the oceans—organisms of organisms. Just as molecules became cells, cells became colonies, and colonies became creatures, now creatures settled into ecosystems.

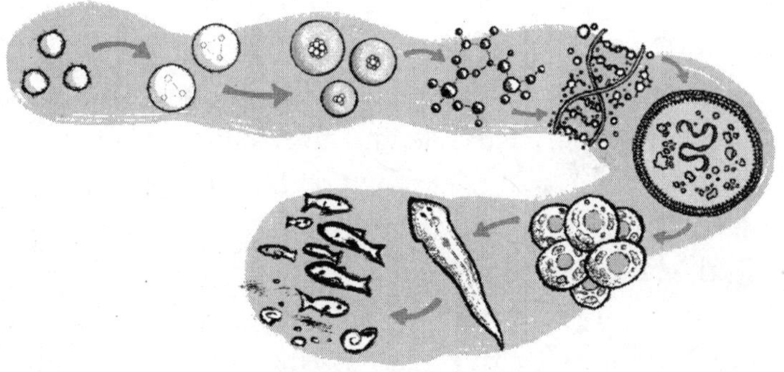

For a massive chunk of Earth's history, the most advanced mode of transport was the ancient waggling flagellum used by bacteria and archaea. But around 425 million years ago, millipedes began to scurry on land with their delicate spindle legs. Fins began to evolve on primitive fish 375 million years ago, and it wasn't long before those fins morphed into the first land-worthy limbs.

That historic first footprint on land, our evolutionary "Seal Armstrong" moment, occurred about 360 million years ago—1.6 galactic birthdays back in history—and was planted by a three-foot-long four-legged fish-descended creature known as *Tiktaalik*.

It wasn't too estranged from us modern humans; it had five-fingered hands and five-toed feet. Our two bodies shared a feature known as the *branchial arches*; in fish, those supported the gills, and in mammals, they held the jawline and voice box.

And those millipedes who first scuttled on land arrived along with the insects, who took to the skies about 325 million years ago in the distant times of the Carboniferous period. In that era, huge heaps of carbon settled deep underneath the ground as long-dead creatures decayed and decomposed into fossil fuel, not to be touched for another 325 million years.

Insects and humans share an ancestor who lived about a billion years ago, leaving us both with 60% of our genetic code. But just like we belong to an extended family of mammals, insects have in-laws in the family of arthropods, which have taken up a family obsession for blood at least 21 times independently—a kind of checkpoint for insect vengeance, at least. Thanks to the odd habit of blood-sucking mouthparts evolving by random chance, our dearest frenemies, the mosquitoes, arrived on the stage around 217 million years ago—about one galactic birthday before today. One spin of our Milky Way later, and you'd be reading a book about it.

When the Earth last crossed this exact region of the galaxy, it was unrecognizable. Every continent was fused into the globe-spanning landmass of *Pangaea*. Our planet was reeling in the hot aftermath of the Permian-Triassic extinction—a volcanic hellscape scene that singlehandedly wiped out 96% of all marine life—nine tenths of life as a whole. Dinosaurs were making their debut on the world stage, and couldn't have cared less about mass extinction events.

What a difference a year makes—especially when it's a galactic one. As we flash past our most recent galactic birthday, we'll need to get more precise—so in the style of Carl Sagan, let's split this last galactic year into 365 galactic days, each about 620,000 Earth years long, and see where that lands us.

Insects were the first to stumble on the utility of wing-powered flight, but they weren't the last. Later, with wings that outspanned the width of a tennis court, the *pterosaurs* arrived with a separately-evolved knack for flight around 215 million years ago, setting the scene near the dawn of the dinosaurs, 330 galactic days ago.

Later on, even mammals hit upon wings; bats developed flight despite having absolutely no link to old insects or giant extinct flying reptiles. For obvious reasons, birds evolved their own wings as well, but not from the pterosaurs. Birds weren't even remotely related.

Birds evolved from *theropods*, a dinosaur family that included T-rex and the velociraptor. It's a sheer coincidence that birds—the direct descendants of two-legged hobbling dinosaurs—even evolved wings *at all*. Pterosaurs and pterodactyls weren't even *true* dinosaurs, despite what children's books continue to spout. Chickens, on the other hand, are.

Of course, about 65 million years ago—a quick 95 galactic days ago on our timeline—the dinosaurs were rudely interrupted by a fifteen-kilometre-wide asteroid, sniping them out of existence in the Cretaceous-tertiary mass extinction event. This was indisputably the highest ratio of birds-to-one-stone in all history.

But with the supreme dinosaurs swept clean from the plate, that asteroid cleared the path for a new group of animals to take centre-stage on our timeline. Thanks to that impact, our direct ancestors, five million generations ago, were able to thrive.

The Cosmic Sniping Range

Dinosaurs were simply unlucky to have been eradicated in their heyday by an asteroid, but rocks aside, there's an even gentler killer out there. Our planet is a shining beacon of life, and yet we're entirely at the whims of a galactic sniping range that trains its crosshairs on our delicate Earth every 62 million years.

This strange pattern was noted in a 2005 California paper by Robert Muller and Rovers Rhode, and it seems to be pretty incessant. While plotting out the total number of living creatures across the ages, a telltale killing spree went down 55 million years ago, decimating a tenth of all life in one fell swoop.

It mirrored the effects of another massacre that struck our planet 117 million years ago, hitting hard for sea sponges, coral reefs, and arthropods alike. Stretch Earth's timeline all the way back to the ruckus of the Cambrian, and you'll see this murder mystery on repeat.

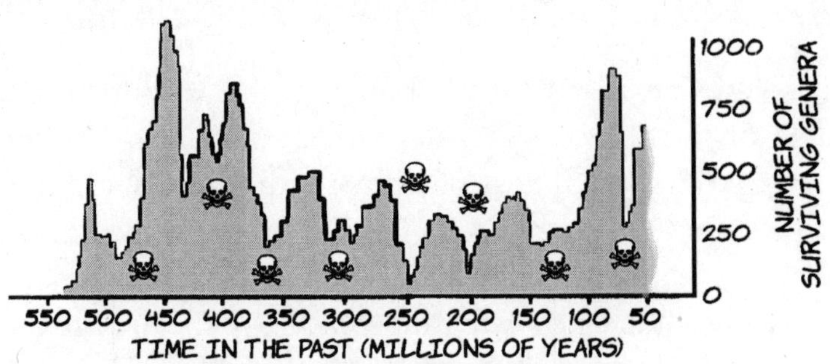

ROHDE, R. MULLER, R. CYCLES IN FOSSIL DIVERSITY. NATURE 434, 208-210 (2005). HTTPS://DOI.ORG/10.1038/NATURE03339

Unlike most causes of death on Earth, this cyclic demise might not come from the Earth at all. Our universe is filled with an arena of lethal cosmic radiation—and it isn't your everyday, run-of-the-mill cancerous radiation; this is a storm of subatomic bullets that can pierce a kilometre into solid bedrock, three kilometres into liquid water, and straight through the delicate rungs of our DNA like a chainsaw through tissue paper.

It's not a fun time, to say the least.

Fortunately for us, the Milky Way galaxy screens us behind an enormous magnetic field, shielding us from cosmic rays like an oversized umbrella. Unfortunately for us, our solar system seems to bob upward and downward in its orbit around the galaxy, sending us careening into that radiation zone about every 62 million years.

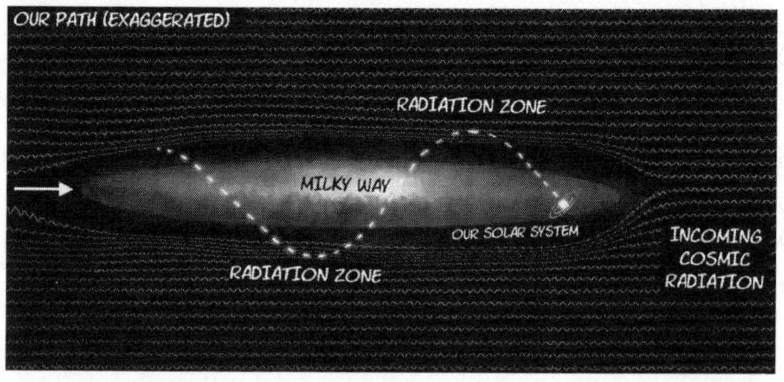

And that means, while bobbing like an intoxicated fish on a rollercoaster ride, our solar system is often scoured in a lethal dose of cosmic radiation. In addition to scrambling the genetic codes of all living beings on Earth, this radiation decimates our sun-shield.

Three-quarters of our atmosphere is made of nitrogen gas (N_2) which is totally harmless. But when it's struck with bolts of cosmic radiation, the nitrogens split, bonding with oxygen to create nitrous oxide (N_2O), which destroys molecules of ozone. The ozone layer just so happens to be our bulletproof vest against the Sun's ultraviolet rays. When it disintegrates, so too goes our safety blanket.

For most species, radiation-tanning is never fun. But for the survivors, cosmic rays can trigger mutations that set life on an entirely new pathway, sometimes for the better.

Nocturnal bats, the cutest rodents of all, evolved their own night-vision goggles about 52 million years ago with the devious art of echolocation. Rather than scooping up night-light with oversized eyes, bats found it helpful to scream in all directions, often at the piercing frequency of 50,000 Hz, then listen to the echo as it ricocheted around them. With their attuned precision, bats can see objects with nothing but reflected sound—kind of like an adorable, fur-coated radar detector.

Fast-forward 22 million years, dolphins evolved the exact same echolocation mechanism in the depths of the oceans—and dolphins are about as similar to bats as Hip-Hop is to classical Mozart.

This is just another freak-accident of convergent evolution. In a 2013 London paper by Joe Parker and colleagues, bats and dolphins both contained the same 200 identical genes linked to echolocation, stitched intricately into their genetic code, all evolved on their separate branches.

An explosion of greenness rocked the world about 21 million years ago, when plans cracked

C4 photosynthesis. It was an alternate brand of the ancient C3 photosynthesis used by cyanobacteria, and it allowed plants to essentially stockpile and pool-up their carbon dioxide reserves, keeping their thirst for sunlight quenched even when the air was parched. C4 photosynthesis evolved 62 times across the world, hitting every corner of the planet—another natural checkpoint of life. From milkweed to quinoa, wheat to rice and corn, it laid out many of the crops we'd later be enjoying on our dinner plates.

Our fellow red-headed orangutangs split from our branch around 16 million years ago—just 23 galactic days ago—and even though about a million generations have passed since then, their cells still contain 97% of our genome.

When they branched off, the great apes arrived on the scene.

Monkey business was surprisingly civilized for its time. Gorillas trooped together into organized social groups, led in chief by a white-furred silverback. Having silver hairs on your back was, in gorilla culture, as kindred to royalty as wearing glasses are to us nerds.

When primatologist Jane Goodall first studied the chimpanzees living in Tanzania, she discovered their habits with tools; it completely upstaged our entire view on humans—a species which, until then, we rashly assumed was the only toolmaker on the planet. Those chimpanzees still pack 98.8% of our genome in their cells. We're so similar that author Terry Pratchett even proposed lumping our species in with them, cheekily calling us *Pan narrans*—the storytelling chimps.

About six million years ago—just 4.5 galactic days behind us—the chimpanzees split, leaving us and a loose crowd of eight doppelgänger species to roam this planet—our closest genetic cousins. They were once the last tendrils on our branch of the tree of life. Only one of those species is still alive today, and it's us.

Planet of the Ape-Descendants

Despite our early genius, humans began their stint on Earth as a critically-endangered species by our modern standards, hard-pressed to the brink of extinction about 900,000 years ago. From fossil records across Asia, Europe and Africa, our grand global population topped out at 1,280 mature humans on Earth. Our lives delicately hung in the balance thanks to a climate crisis that went down in the mid-Pleistocene era.

If aliens had surveyed our Earth back then, I doubt they'd have bet the galactic equivalent of a dollar on the notion that this pitiful ape-descendant creature would someday rule the planet with a mighty population of eight billion and counting.

We did survive, for better or worse, and thanks to that, our future was paved for modern humans along with our extinct cousins, the Neanderthals. But what got us through that harrowing crisis? Probably random chance, if we're being serious. But I'd argue that sheer kindness gave us a fighting chance.

Nature was a brutal place for our ancestors, and if you lost your ability to shred and gobble up meat, the wrath of starvation would soon pluck you out. But in 2005, a fossilized corpse from one of our primate ancestors was excavated in Georgia.

This dead fellow, a four-foot-tall male, walked the world about 1.7 million years ago with almost no teeth. When his remains were found at the *Dmanisi* archaeological site, his skull had just one surviving tooth; the fossil itself wasn't broken. He'd survived this way, living to the ripe age of forty—and bear in mind, that age would have qualified you for *extreme* senior benefits in Palaeolithic times.

Robbed of the ability to chew meat, this person's survival was almost certainly tied to the care and compassion of his tribe. Before humans ever entered the world stage, kindness was pervading our ancestors.

Around 45,000 years ago, the fossil of a Neanderthal man was dug up near Kurdistan. His skull was severely beaten, bashed on the left side; his left eye was totally destroyed; his right arm was likely paralyzed; his right leg was damaged and crippled; his foot was shattered. But those injuries weren't fresh; he'd survived to the impressive age of 45 in that sorry condition.

It's hard to imagine how he could've lived so long without the compassion of his tribe. Was he bringing some grand survival advantage to the clan? Perhaps his life was valued enough, just as it was, to keep around.

Nobody's ever patented fire, mostly because no one was flame-retardant enough to carry it into the clerk's office and survive long enough to sign the filing documents. Yet, the tools that ignited it are still one of humanity's finest inventions.

Those earliest relics of fire were scavenged up at the *Daughters of Jacob Bridge* in Israel, clocking back 790,000 years, scarcely 1.3 galactic days, into our past. For the first time ever, our ancestors cooked meat around a campfire. Fire endowed us with more than on-demand heat. It cast light; our hands cast shadows; human stories were born.

We humans weren't the only brainiac species in town. Neanderthals had a knack for smarts too, boasting a brain of similar size. Their species was so related to us, matching with 99% of our genome, that Neanderthals upheld several *human* traditions long before humans ever did. Iraq's *Shanidar Cave* holds the first graveyards and burial sites ever to emerge on Earth—but those graves don't belong to us. Over 150,000 years ago, Neanderthals held rituals for their deceased; we humans only fancied that idea 15,000 years ago, at *Taforalt Cave* in Morocco.

Neanderthals once used a small rock tool called the Mousterian, a hallmark trace of their presence. Back in 2012, those rocks were spotted on Crete—an island 160 kilometres south of mainland Greece, by George Ferentinos and colleagues. It's unlikely that the Neanderthals *swam* there, but if they once roamed that island, how could they possibly have gotten ashore?

Ferentinos posed the striking idea that Neanderthals, over a hundred millennia before human yachts and ferries ever putted on the water, had already mastered the craft of sailing—basic ships compared to ours, but still a serious shot at spooning across the waters, traversing two patches of land that stood a practical universe apart. If Ferentinos is correct, then our inaugural maritime cruise came here, about 130,000 years ago, taken not by us, but by a curious species resembling us in almost every way.

It wasn't just Crete; deep within the fossilized soils of islands around the world, there's a common relic of ours: *Oldowan* rocks—the oldest tools our ancestors ever used. They've been dug up in 2004 on the islands of Flores and Sulawesi, north of Australia; in 2008 on the island of Socotra, East of Africa; and in 2009 on the island of Luzon, south of Asia.

Those relics all clock over 800,000 years back in time—and keep in mind, those islands aren't a mere skip across a duck pond. You'd need to sail across 200 kilometres of open seas to wash up on their shores. In terms of our textbook portrayal of our ancestors, that's a sea-change.

We've always seen ourselves as a bunch of landlubbers: a species keen to kiss the earth and hobble across deserts and mountains; a species who only had the gall to jump in a boat a few thousand years ago. But it's possible that we've been sailing on chunks of driftwood with gusto ever since we evolved the brains to ride them.

Ancient relics of Neanderthals and their culture rest at *Grotte du Renne* cave in France, and there's even evidence that a raving fashion trend swept across Neanderthals in Europe some 50,000 years ago, adorning their bodies in feathers, coloured pigments, shells, and teeth. It was fast fashion for an incredibly slow age.

Whatever styles and crazes befell the Neanderthals, it came to an end around 41,000 years ago when their entire species died out. There's still a cloud of mystery around *how* they went extinct, but it almost certainly involved us. Whether it was an outright bloodshed battle, a lack of resources, or just a lack of mates thanks to their habit of interbreeding with us humans, Neanderthals vanished just 1.6 galactic hours ago on our timeline.

Humans have stood alone ever since.

We're a diverse species, scattered to every corner of Earth, but if you trace back our billions of family trees, they're all connected to one person in the savannah of East Africa some 155,000 years ago. Her name, *Mitochondrial Eve*, owes itself to the fact that she's an ancestor to every living human, linked in an unbroken family lineage. We know nothing else about her, just that she existed—and that we all inherited her mitochondria.

The powerhouses of our cells do divide, but they don't breed like we do. Male and female sex cells get mixed and blended in the genetic mayhem of human mating, but our mitochondria don't scramble their genetics; they're only passed down through females, so their genome simply gets copied and pasted. In other words, mitochondria hold some of the finest DNA on the planet, not tampered or fettered by mating.

In the 1970s, geneticist Rebecca Cann took genetic samples from the mitochondria of women across the world. From the genes they all shared between them, she and her colleagues pinpointed *Mitochondrial Eve* at the root of our family tree.

And the amount of genes we all share in common: 99.92%.

That's 1/1300th of a genome's difference across all humans.

That's just a number, sure, but it's worth a reckoning. Across our stained human history, think for a second about all those battles and wars, squabbles of blind hatred, and crusades hailed against nations—all justified, at least by some people across history, on the basis of their enemies being 1/1300th of a genome apart.

Our fascination with violence is about as old as our obsession with immortality. We've made no progress

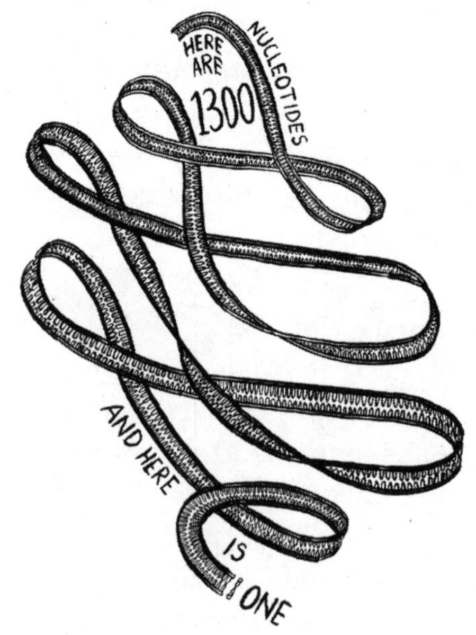

on finding fanciful items like the philosopher's stone, the fountain of youth, or some elixir of life, but 51,000 years ago—about two galactic hours in the past—we did reckon a pretty ingenious way to cheat death.

This reckoning was just a smudge of paint etched onto the walls of a cave on the island of Sulawesi in Indonesia. The walls hold an ancient portrait of a pig surrounded by people.

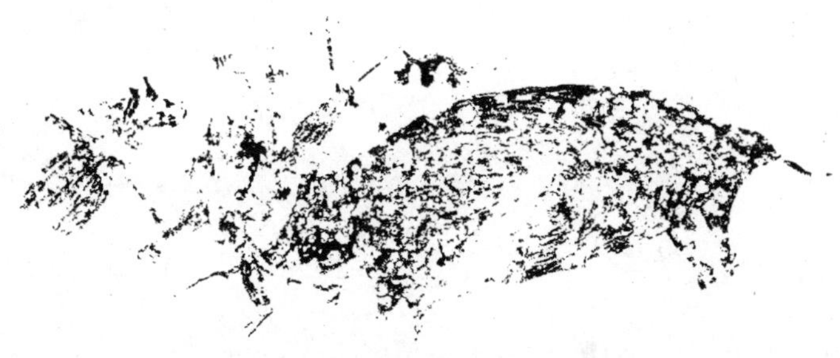

Its meaning isn't exactly clear, but it marked a profound shift in our view of the world. For the first time, humans left more than a pile of fermented fossils behind; we left a message, a story, a purpose. Our thoughts erupted past our petty death-obsessed brains and onto a timeless canvas of rock. We learned to outlive our own lifespans by downloading our ideas from flesh to surface. Nowadays, we call that stunt publishing.

Alongside those prime artists, the first math nerds arrived on the scene 46,000 years ago at *Border Cave* in South Africa. Burrowed in that cave was a fanciful set of tick-marked bones. The exact source of these bones is unknown—but whoever's bones they once were, they served as a blackboard on which we first dabbled in counting.

The last global ice age wracked our planet about 25,000 years ago—and it's been scarcely 50 galactic minutes

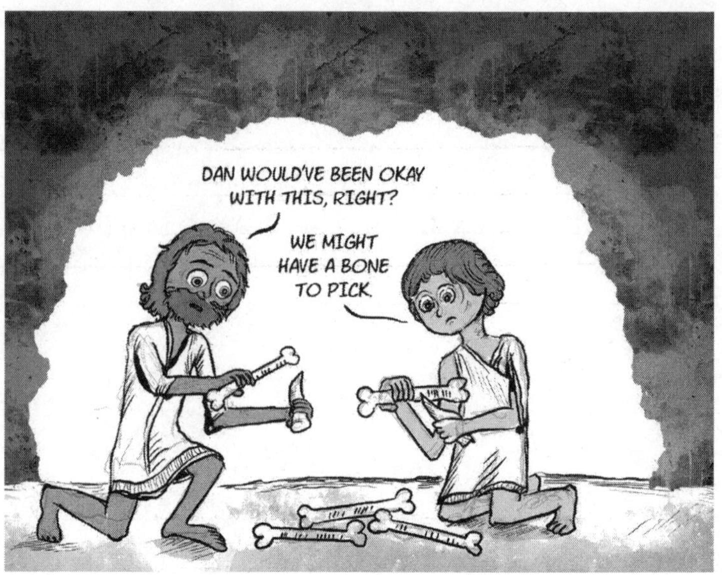

since then. Freezing up a bridge between East Asia and North America—an entire swath of this planet we hadn't even laid feet upon until that historic migration. With a steadfast curiosity, we crossed that continental bridge around 13,500 years ago.

In that same chapter of time, across the world in the Middle East, the Natufian peoples began building up the first villages in the world. In the lush backwash of the most recent ice age, farming was kickstarted in Mesopotamia just 12,000 years or 28 galactic minutes ago, landing an entrée of wheat and barley on the prehistoric menu.

This menu marked the start of the Neolithic Revolution—a lifestyle shift that took the entire world by storm. With the dawn of farming, most of humanity shunned the hunter-gatherer life in favour of huge towns and fields stocked with crops.

And the rest is history—literally.

From Caves to the Cosmos

People advise us to study history or find ourselves repeating it. History textbook editors clearly don't get this, because while new textbook editions keep dropping, their tone of writing hasn't changed in over a century, still gracing our schools with a dialect that comes across as drier than breadcrumbs. For that reason, it's long overdue for history to be told with a different spin.

Long ago, molecules joined up to survive as cells, cells bonded into colonies, colonies into creatures, creatures into tribes, and now tribes joined to forge societies. On our huge galactic timeline, we darted across the entire history of civilization over the span of a lunch break—about 25 minutes at most.

One of humanity's first major settlements was Çatalhöyük, rising in 7100 BCE, less than 22 galactic minutes back in history. It sported a boxed-up rookery of houses which clustered into a single network—no long tendrils of roads weaved between the homes, as those cities evolved later.

Çatalhöyük hosted one of the world's first economies; its citizens didn't have to be know-all survivalists anymore. Instead, they were able to specialize at their various jobs, each doing their unique bit to keep the city alive. The settlement brought a myriad of carpenters, farmers, teachers, sculptors, and jewellers—and peer pressure became a thing for humans too.

But most unique of all, Çatalhöyük brought the domestication of animals on a city-wide level. Rather than totally devouring the lambs, goats and cattle that lived amongst them, they struck a bond. The animals nurtured the inhabitants with milk—and maybe the occasional meat-steak—and Çatalhöyük offered them a safe grazing residence.

And so farms, the powerhouses of society, were born.

In rapid-fire succession, societies blew up worldwide: in Mesopotamia just 6,500 years ago—a mere 15 minutes ago on our galactic timeline—then in India and Egypt 13 minutes ago, and China 12 minutes ago.

The ancient *cuneiform script* was etched upon stones just 11 minutes ago, ushering in the age of writing. Humans gained the ability to implant their ideas on clay and toss words millennia into the future, where we'd one day receive their written echoes. The number *pi* first came to mind around this time, spearheading our search for a language of nature.

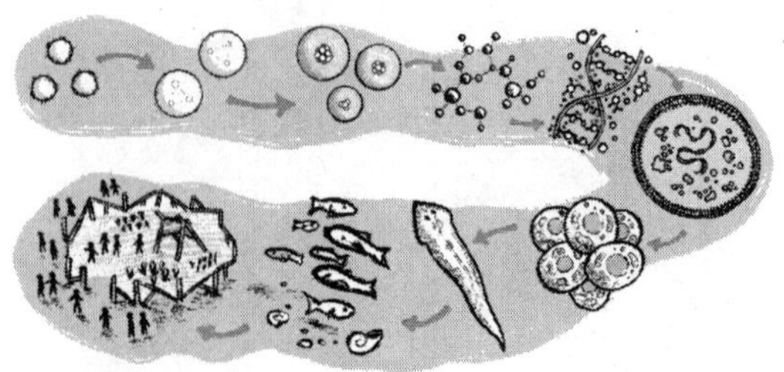

The first foreign armies began to pierce into new territories around 2250 BCE when a fellow named *Sargon of Akkad* lay siege upon ancient Mesopotamia and conquered what's now known as Syria and Iran. It was a new threat, armies and battalions and such, that only arose once we lived together in cities, and since each person was ill-equipped to fight and survive alone, a new job began to specialize: national defence.

Armies popped up in China 4,200 years ago, Egypt 3,900 years ago, and India 3,800 years ago. It was an immune system for nations, kept in business not with cytokines, but money—a concept that was fashioned into existence around 2150 BCE with the Mesopotamian shekel.

Our first human sailboats darted across the Tigris and Euphrates Rivers as the Sumerians embarked onto water around 3000 BCE; the Egyptians sailed down to Ethiopia soon after, while the Chinese followed with their own waterborne sails around 500 years later. The oceans forced us apart no longer.

When the Polynesians first crafted seaworthy boats around 1300 BCE, their wayfinding skills carried their boats across the Pacific Ocean, making landfall in Hawaii and New Zealand, the Samoan and Tongan islands, the coast of Tuvalu and Gambier, and over a thousand islands spanning as far eastward as Rapa Nui.

This was humanity's first odyssey into the wide unknown; never had a culture settled the islands of an entire ocean before. With a grand 36 million km^2 between their island chains, not a single empire in the world came close to rivalling what the Polynesians settled.

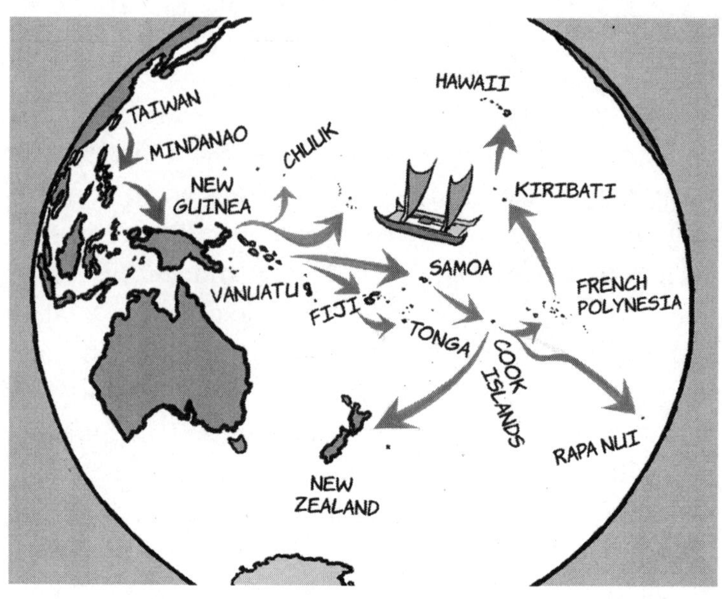

The ancient Polynesians used a navigation tool known as the *titiro ʻētū*—a round coconut shell that tracked the stars as they shifted in latitude. The ships sailed south, and the stars drifted north; the coconut turned to match it. These people might have known our planet was spherical over a thousand years before the Greeks earned their spotlight credit for realizing the exact same thing—when the philosopher Eratosthenes pegged two poles in the ground, about 500 kilometres apart, and saw two curved shadows.

Even 3,400 years ago, an ancestor to everyone currently alive today had probably already been born. We've all got a biological family tree—two parents, four grandparents, eight great-grandparents, and so on—but the pattern can't grow forever. Keep on doubling your grannies and gramps every generation, and just 33 generations back, your ancestors apparently outnumbered the entire population of the world—which is obviously a bit absurd.

But your family tree isn't *separate* from everyone else's; you have siblings who share your parents, cousins who share your grandparents, and second-cousins who share your great-grandparents, intertwining the roots of *your* family tree and *theirs*. Those grandparents had their own siblings, cousins, and second-cousins, intermingling the whole tree even more.

And nobody really cares if you have kids with your twenty-fourth cousin; it happens all the time. So eventually, it's less of a family tree, and more of a long winding lacework of distant forlorn cousins. Dial the clocks back far enough, and most people—even total strangers—don't just share *some* of your ancestors, but *all* of them.

In 1999, mathematician Joseph Chang calculated, with near certainty, that someone lived around 3,000 to 3,400 years ago at the tip of humanity's modern family tree. Whoever they were, they're the last person to own a slot in the family trees of *everyone* alive today. From them, we're all fiftieth-cousins or closer, meaning *family* gatherings are technically *all* gatherings.

The modern Gregorian calendar (the one that's currently marked at 2025) began to tick a mere 4.7 galactic minutes ago, kicking off a short while after the Parthians sacked ancient Rome, setting in motion a long-drawn-out squabble lasting 30 seconds on our timescale. Nine seconds later, the Romans sacked the Sassanians, who then sacked the Byzantines 44 seconds hence, who themselves sacked the Bulgarians 11 seconds later. Over the next six seconds, Bulgaria sacked back, but was subsequently sacked by the Ottomans 20 seconds down the line; the Ottomans then sacked Persia some 15 seconds later.

On our galactic timeline, our history is soaked in sacked blood.

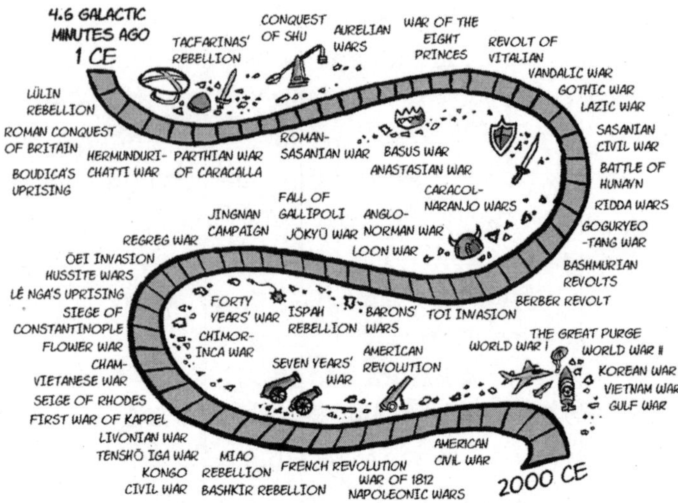

A BRIEF HISTORY OF HUMANS SACKING ONE ANOTHER

The astronomer Hypatia, who ascended to fame in Greece around 400 CE, was a pioneer in her work in mapping star charts and the motions of planets. You'd think Greece might have eschewed the whole sacking frenzy, but Hypatia was stoned to death by a religious mob, thanks to her pagan beliefs.

Following a millennium of sack-backs, Italy fell under the iron-fisted rule of the Roman Inquisition, with a zero-tolerance policy for heretical ideas. Back in 1584, about 62 seconds ago on our timeline, the Italian philosopher Giordano Bruno first put forth the idea that our universe could be infinite, that distant stars might host their own planets, and that those planets might just harbour their own life. He wasn't too well-received by the Inquisition; in fact, the only people to whom Bruno was really well-received were the executioners at the Campo de' Fiori who burned him alive.

In France, slightly earlier in 1553, the early physician Michael Servetus was the first to describe our circulatory system—an unholy mishmash of tubes and tissues and flesh rather than a divine aura of holistic magic. The Calvinist authorities were less than thrilled by his beliefs, and Servetus earned the same burning treatment as Bruno. Tied to a wooden dowel, he once again allowed the executioner to turn a prophet.

Galileo fashioned his first telescope 52 seconds ago, aiming it up at Jupiter and spotting its four moons. He would have escaped the sack-a-thon of history were it not for his decision to preach the revolutionary new idea that perhaps the Earth *did* revolve around the Sun. That landed him under house arrest for the remainder of his life.

Believing science and scientists hasn't exactly been our forte across history. Thanks to our evolution, despite our unrivalled brains and four thousand years of science, we humans have a remarkable knack for tossing evidence out the window.

It's not anyone's fault in particular. The amygdala—the region of our brain which judges if we're about to be chomped by a lion, skewered by an enemy, or just generally put in mortal peril—has advanced in size and structure by less than 5% since the dawn of our species, back in those olden days where clinging to a tribe was absolutely essential for survival, and opting for the loner lifestyle was practically synonymous with volunteering to become a lion's lunch.

Thanks to the weeding process of survival of the fittest, those tribe-loving habits grew to encompass just about everyone. If enough of the folks in your group believed a certain legend or story to explain the world, your membership in that group depended on *you* believing it too.

Thanks to that subscribe-or-die mentality, abandoning your tribe's beliefs was about as senseless as stepping out into a lion's den. From peer pressure to self-esteem, our minds are still locked and loaded with a set of instincts that served us awesomely in the wilderness, but simply crippled us with biases when it came to mingling with modern apes in a modern society—which is where we're at now.

Can we really blame people for that?

On our galactic birthday timeline, everything that's gone down since the end of the Renaissance fits snugly into a single galactic minute—quick enough to miss it while brushing your teeth. France fell into the anarchy of the French Revolution 32 seconds ago, and one second later, the Industrial Revolution saw its first steam engine train clack down a railroad in Wales.

Steam engines were ushered in as the hottest new gadgets; our society fell in love with coal, burning it to power our trains and ships, heat our homes, light our streetlamps, power our stovetops, and crank our factories. Little did we know this hellbent fixation on coal was blasting billions of tons of carbon dioxide into the atmosphere.

For a while, the oceans soaked up the excess supply. Seawater is basically a pond of H_2O molecules, and when carbon dioxide (CO_2) mixes in, their atoms jostle around and regroup into carbonic acid (H_2CO_3). Some of that acid transforms into calcium carbonate ($CaCO_3$) which has a fantastically stable shelf-life as a sandy white sediment that stains the crevices of the seafloor.

As our world charioted full speed ahead in its fervour over oil and coal, even the oceans couldn't store the full load of carbon dioxide, and our skies began to pollute in our own kind of Great Carbonization Event—and since CO_2 is so much better than oxygen at sponging our Sun's heat, the atmosphere began to uptick in temperature.

If you're a cyanobacterium, it was around now that you felt that huge rush of nostalgia—a sudden flash of déjà vu you thought you'd never feel again. If you're *not* a cyanobacterium, it was around now that you began to panic.

With rising temperatures, the polar ice caps weren't thrilled; ice reflects sunlight; less ice, more sunlight; more sunlight, more heat; more heat, less ice. Just like Mikhail Budyko worked out the runaway deep-freeze that wracked our planet 700 million years ago, we've been tempting fate with a runaway hot-flash.

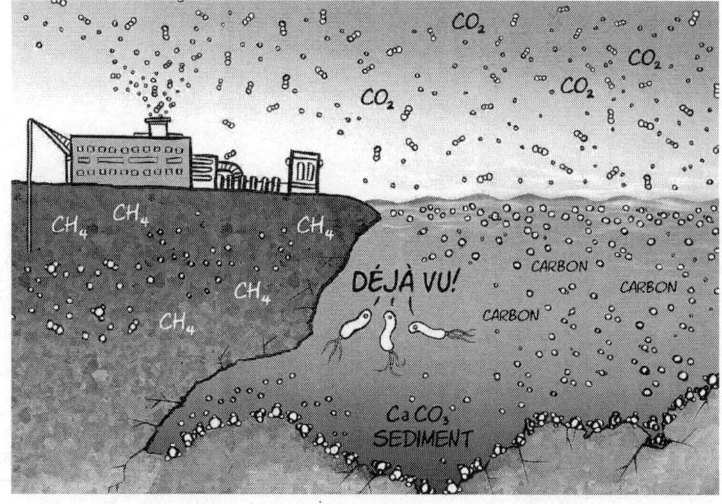

Even back in 1856, the American scientist Eunice Foote had discovered the fact that CO_2 was capable of turning our skies into a sauna. Her experiment, which placed four canisters of gas in the sunlight, had drawn obvious attention to carbon dioxide, which heated up most of all. Her work was forgotten for over a century—but it was hauntingly accurate.

Skip ahead to 1896, and the Swedish scientist Svante Arrhenius spent a year calculating the effects of doubling the carbon dioxide in our skies. His graphs pitted our planet on a pathway to warm up to 6°C beyond its natural threshold if humanity let it slip.

He published his work in a rapt depression, but his misery wasn't from the existential threat of climate change he'd just foreseen on his paper; it was instead because, as he admitted, it was "unbelievable that so trifling a matter [had] cost [him] a full year."

And well, what a trifling matter it turned out to be indeed.

If our fellow cyanobacteria have taught us anything, it's that Earth's environment *kind of bites* when the whole atmosphere gets overhauled. If we let it slip, the Intergovernmental Panel on Climate Change has listed over 2.6 million species at risk of extinction. That's 2.6 million branches on the tree of life, each with its own four-billion-year-long backstory as outrageous as ours. That's a grand total of 110 quadrillion years of life's evolution in our hands—over eight million universes of clocked-up time, all on this one little world.

But unlike the world that Foote and Arrhenius knew, we're striding into this century with an arsenal of climate solutions—more than we've ever known before. A depot of four million wind turbines could run our planet, same with a 300 km^2 blanket of solar panels. Climatologist Jeremy Munday, in a 2019 Maryland paper, even proposed coating our cities in a palette of ultra-white paint to reflect more sunlight, effectively returning Earth to something like its frosted goth era. Back in the Cryogenian period, 700 million years ago, the Earth was cool before it was cool.

Humanity was plunged into the devastation of World War I just 16 galactic seconds ago, followed two seconds later by World War II. In that six-second window of our galactic timeline, more people were killed than the entire world population ever was for 98% of human history. An entire prehistoric Earth's worth of humans, gone—all over 0.08% of a genome's variance.

But that same century, our species took its first strides into the cosmos. The first satellite, *Sputnik I*, circled overhead just nine galactic seconds ago. With the touchdown of *Apollo 11* back in 1969, we stamped our first footprints on lunar soil. Over the next galactic second, we landed ten spacecraft on Venus, three on Mars, five more crews of people on the Moon, and to round it off, we delivered four messages in cosmic bottles.

We launched the *Pioneer* and *Voyager* probes—our first greeting calls into the galactic wilderness—hoping that one day, some curious alien fellow in the universe might pick it up.

Just like the Sumerians and Egyptians made their own first contact over 5,500 years ago, our whole planet sent its first messengers into the galactic desert in 1972. Those probes were our first shot at speaking the language of the stars.

The Language of the Stars

Imagine you've been tasked with mailing a letter to a friend whose only language is more foreign to you than Shakespeare is to a hamster. Without the thankless assistance of Duolingo or Google Translate, how would you direct-message this fellow to tell them about your culture, the planet you inhabit, and your species? They've never known a smidge of your society, your memes, your poetry, customs or traditions—and they're not too enthusiastic about a meetup, given that their home is over a dozen trillion kilometers away. What lingo could you possibly both understand?

NASA was preoccupied by this conundrum in 1972 as it neared the historic launch of the *Pioneer 10* and *Pioneer 11* spacecraft.

Those two space missions aimed to slingshot past the outer planets of Jupiter and Saturn, sending us back a mountain of new data. But scientists knew these probes weren't coming back. Their orbits would slingshot them up to 65,000 kilometres per hour, enough to slip the bounds of the Sun's gravitational riptide and sail into the galactic void forever.

Knowing this, the astronomer Carl Sagan suggested that a little message get tagged onto the probes—a cosmic greeting from the human race. In one of the narrowest deadlines in rocket science history, Sagan had three weeks to compose a message with artist Linda Salzman and astronomer Frank Drake. Scrawled onto a gold plaque, that message became like humanity's first profile picture in the cosmic group chat. It was our first intentional alien-coded message.

But how could humans—a species who often can't even make sense of smalltalk in *their own* language—be capable of communicating to an alien creature who likely knows less about human behavior than a muppet?

If we ever made contact with alien life, would humans fall flat on our faces in a fruitless attempt to speak in some daft language of the stars, or might we find a lot more in common than we think?

For simplicity's sake, Carl Sagan swept aside all culture and politics. If you've seen the media lately, or basically ever, you'll know that we're capable of babbling and rambling on about that for decades. Sagan wanted to convey just one simple message on the plaque: where we live, and what we are.

It's hard to mail your cosmic address into space when none of your recipients know what a postal code is, but we found a method using *pulsars*, the fast-spinning husks of long-exploded dead stars.

These beacons were discovered in 1967 when astronomer Jocelyn Bell Burnell noticed a telltale blinking pattern in the skies. Like cosmic lighthouses, pulsars shine two twirling beams of light into the universe. We mapped those as our reference points, which is like mailing your home address in relation to the nearest graveyards. I do it all the time.

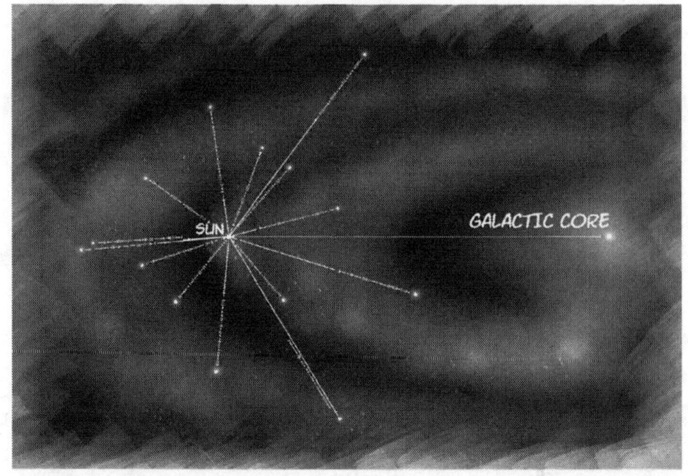

On the *Pioneer* plaque, we're posing proud and naked—at least, the outline of a human male and female were etched as such. There was no shame in putting it on humanity's cosmic profile, since no one reading it would have a clue what human clothes looked like in the first place. The hardest part was conveying the *height* of humans. We didn't want to seem like Godzilla, nor did we want to come across as seven-inch hobbits.

Finding a common yardstick is hard enough *here on Earth*—as the United States still clings to the imperial system in spite of the rest of the world flaunting the metric system and its charm. Alien life would live in blissful ignorance of both systems, having no clue what a foot or a metre means, nor the reason we squabble over them so much.

To set the universal yardstick, Carl Sagan chose 21.106 centimetres. You might imagine he selected this number by throwing a dart while blindfolded, but this specific value was *carefully* chosen. It's a peculiar property of the most common atom in existence.

In 1951, the astronomers Edward Purcell and Harold Ewen identified the source of an odd buzz of radio waves emanating across our galaxy like a music channel being broadcast in every corner of the universe.

These radio waves, as it turns out, weren't streaming from any specific location; the kerfuffle was coming from hydrogen floating in empty space, and it had a wavelength of 21.106 centimetres, never more, never less. Try adding *that* unit to the meter-vs-foot debate, and see how much hate mail it earns you.

The source of that radio is hydrogen's single electron, which sometimes flips over like a wobbling spinning top, spitting out a radio wave at one *extremely* specific wavelength. If you're seeking some cosmic jazz, this hydrogen radio broadcast channel is technically *1420.4* and has been downvoted for its mind-numbing static.

Because the speed of light is the cosmic speed limit, and because hydrogen is the most common atom in nature, Carl Sagan set 21.106 centimetres as the cosmic yardstick.

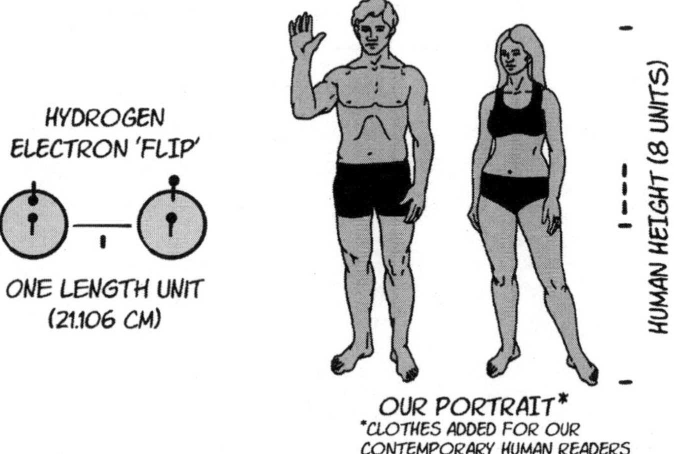

Next to our self-portraits, Sagan added two lines, one at our feet, the other at the female's head. Between those lines, a *line-dash-dash-dash* was written. It's meant to represent the digits 1·0·0·0, the number *eight* in binary code, since the average human female is about eight of those hydrogen-radio yardsticks tall.

We hoped, at the bare minimum, that any civilization with enough nerdom to pluck an alien probe from outer space would at least share our common obsession with math.

Two years after the *Pioneer* probes set sail, we turned our gaze to a more lucrative messaging platform: radio waves. Spacecraft and rockets are fine and dandy, but if we're hoping to send a message in a bottle, we picked a horribly sluggish bottle.

The furthest probe we've ever launched, *Voyager 1*, has been sailing for over fifty years, and it's crossed 0.064% of the distance to Proxima Centauri—the nearest star past our own Sun.

So, in 1974, the *Arecibo Observatory* prepared to beam an interstellar radio message to the star cluster *Messier 13*, a village containing some half-a-million stars, at the speed of light: 17,800 times faster than Voyager 1. Armed with its 305-metre-wide radio dish, Arecibo beamed a binary-coded signal across the universe with the equivalent strength of blasting your car radio at twenty trillion watts—enough to make a semitrailer explode.

Encoded in that string of binary digits was a picture composed of 1,679 pixels which, when stitched together, formed a little pamphlet of the human race—a cosmic greeting call to anyone who might be listening. We chose 1,679 pixels for a reason, not because data quality was trash in the seventies—although, let's be honest, it really was—but rather because the string of binary beeps was utter nonsense until it got boxed into a rectangular picture. The number 1,679 can only be broken down into 23 × 73—two prime numbers—and we hoped aliens would take this as an invitation to stack those pixels 23 columns wide and 73 rows tall.

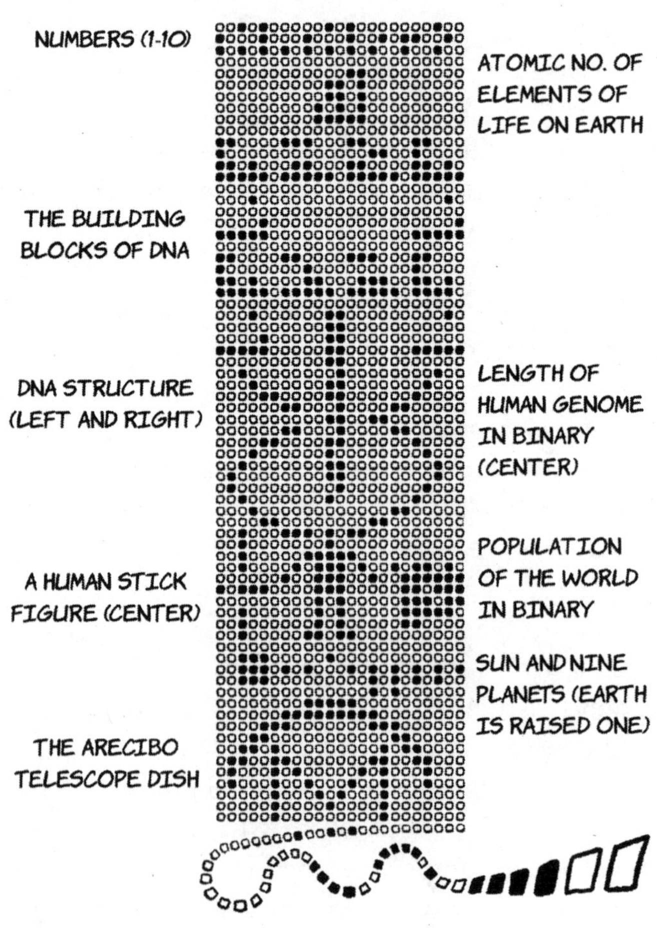

For a species who's often afraid to share their own phone numbers, I'll admit we dumped a *huge* amount of personal info from the Arecibo Observatory—and that's another point: we can toss math and numbers into the universe, but is that *all* that's worth sharing? Sometimes just marvelling at the sheer elegance of our planet's countless cultures, even if certain aspects don't register any hint of sense in our minds, is beautiful. We're not merely a planet of math-addicts. We're a slew of storytellers, musicians, writers, lovers, and generally non-robotic human beings.

Those were the vibes we delivered in 1977 with the launch of the *Voyager 1* and *Voyager 2* space probes; both of them sailed outside our solar system in this last decade. Tucked away on each spacecraft is a copy of the world-famous *Golden Record*, a 54-minute soundtrack from the Earth and its residents.

Summing up *Earth* in under an hour was a daunting task, and Carl Sagan most certainly knew it when he spearheaded the project.

The record holds our greetings in 55 languages. We engraved *shalom* (שלום) and *salaam* (سلام) onto the record, both of them words for peace. We included the sound of a midafternoon breeze. We etched the sounds of birds tweeting, crickets chirping, a human heartbeat, whales calling, a mother kissing her child, and the brainwaves of a human falling in love. Brainwaves, in a deep sense, might be the most basic thing we share in common with other thinking, conscious life forms across the galaxy—a long shot, but perhaps the best we've got.

There's a music sample from Bach's *Brandenburg Concerto*, the indigenous Australian song *Barnumbirr*, the Indonesian folk song *Puspåwarnå*, the American jazz song *Melancholy Blues*, the traditional Indian *Bhairavi*, and 22 other works of Earth's music.

Since the shelf-life of the record is tagged at one billion years before it corrodes into dead metal by cosmic radiation, these musical numbers upstage the entire genre of "timeless oldies" by a factor of 10 million. Those songs will make four complete orbits around the Milky Way in their lifespan. Who knows who might give them a listen.

It's hard to imagine an alien species understanding the record, but maybe that doesn't matter. Perhaps just listening to the whims and wonders of a distant planet is special enough. Even beautiful gibberish can be pretty poetic.

Maybe the *Golden Record* and the *Pioneer Plaque* were less about sending a greeting to aliens, and more a reflection of how we wanted to see ourselves. The missions demanded us to think not in English or French or any one of the world's seven thousand spoken languages, but in a cosmic code that even alien races might decipher one day.

Ever since we've cast messages into the void, we've been checking our cosmic voicemail for replies. We've been scanning our night skies since 1984, when the SETI institute—the *Search for Extraterrestrial Intelligence*—was founded. Its sole mission has been to sweep the galaxy for radio signals in the fleeting chance that amidst the ear-crushing static buzz of a quarter-trillion stars, we might eavesdrop on a cosmic greeting from a distant extraterrestrial civilization curiously calling into the void.

But across five decades, we've heard nothing.

There *have* been a handful of farcical false alarms.

In August 1977, the *Big Ear* radio telescope detected an impressive radio signal in the direction of Sagittarius which was so convincing that astronomer Jerry Ehman circled the data and jotted "*Wow!*" on the page. The *Wow!* signal was never spotted again.

In the mid-2010s, the *Parkes Observatory* in Australia detected a series of quick and flashy radio beeps broadcasting from erratic directions across the galaxy. These beeps persisted for just a few seconds, but were detected continuously for several years—until January 2015, when a team of scientists discovered the true source, a microwave oven in the basement kitchen.

To round it off, in December 2020, one initiative called the *Breakthrough Listen* project picked up a hallmark signal of alien radio intelligence from our nearest celestial neighbour, Proxima Centauri. Two scientific papers and one exhausted team of astronomers later, the source was followed back to a human radio channel on the same frequency. We've seemed to have this incredible knack for *not* finding evidence of alien intelligence.

Perhaps our radio technology is still too primitive. With our finest equipment, we could tune in on Earth's yapping from about 10 light-years away—a laughably small range in a galaxy that's 100,000 light-years across. Our own limitations might make listening for alien radio about as senseless as screaming over a mountain range.

And radio itself might be daftly obsolete for most civilizations—especially since we've only been tinkering with it for one century. By this point, trying to contact advanced aliens with radio might be as naïve as text-messaging a computer scientist with a carrier pigeon. But even if we're using the galactic equivalent of carrier pigeons, still—nobody's mailed us.

For most of us, this galactic silence means nothing. But the astronomer Enrico Fermi took that apparent lack of cosmic texts very seriously. He reasoned that our galaxy has been around for nearly 13 billion years, it's held over a trillion stars in its history, and those stars have hosted families of countless planets—countless shots at cooking up clever life.

He also assumed that an alien civilization, much like humans across our history, would probably have a hellbent drive to expand and colonize every patch of landmass within reach—just ask the British; they'd know.

And considering that our ancestors may have had the guts to travel to the islands of Crete, Socotra, Luzon and Flores *independently*, it's not unreasonable to throw in the wild guess that star-sailing might be a popular sport across the galaxy. With those assumptions, if just *one* alien civilization broke free of the shackles of their home planet and began booking it into space at 10% of the speed of light, they'd be able to settle the entire Milky Way, world for world, in just one million years.

But in Earth's four-billion-year-long history, never once has it been decommissioned and converted to an extraterrestrial pitstop. This stark lack of alien visitors set off an actual scientific debate known as the *Fermi Paradox*. The general gist is this: if civilizations are sprouting up across the cosmos, why the *heck* haven't we spotted them yet?

Just to get a sense of the baffling odds stacked in favour of alien civilizations existing, let's consider a short and quippy equation devised by the astronomer Frank Drake in 1961—a numerical best-guess to estimate how many empires might've teemed across our galaxy over its thirteen-billion-year-long history.

The Milky Way has been evolving since the universe was freshly 800 million years old, and since then, our galaxy has birthed around seven new stars every year. We've got about 200 billion stars in the galaxy today, and based on loose stats from the *Optical Gravitational Lensing Experiment* from 2002-2007, stars are often swamped with a couple planets, averaging about 1.6 worlds per solar system.

If you're brewing life, you'll need a crapload of water. Unless we find an alternate variant of life that spawns in methane or silicon or some alternative brand of chemistry, we're under the assumption that water is the prime ingredient—and perhaps that's too narrow, but for now it's the most we know. Since water-loving life can't exist in boiling steam or solid ice, water needs to be held in that precious range of 0°C→100°C where it trickles as a liquid, which means planets need to orbit at a *very* specific distance from the swelter of their stars.

You're probably well-familiar with this effect while in the shower. As we all know, there is one *infinitesimal* location on the heat dial of a shower that's survivable to its human occupants. Turn the dial a millimetre to the left, and you're boiled alive; a millimetre to the right, and you freeze solid. For the planetary equivalent of a shower, this is known as the *habitable zone*, and in 2017, the Kepler space telescope and Keck Observatory predicted that 14% of all rocky planets in the universe lie within it.

Now let's suppose, from all the water-swamped worlds in our galaxy, that 1-in-1000 actually does evolve life, and from those rare life-breeding planets, let's assume that 10% of them evolve intelligent brains. From those rare brain-infested worlds, let's say that 10% produce life clever enough to crack radio technology and beam signals into space. Your typical mammalian species has an evolutionary shelf-life of around seven million years; let's toss in a random guess that civilizations expire after that long, too.

Summing up the grand total, we could expect around 650,000 civilizations to have risen across our galaxy's history, with 103 members active in the cosmic group chat right now.

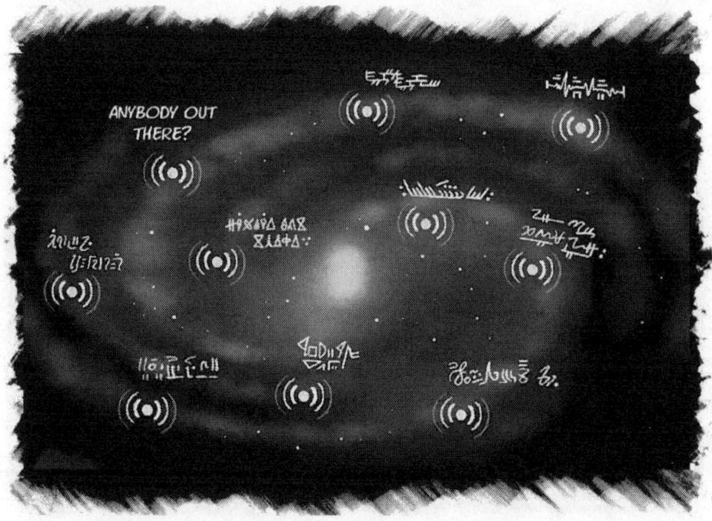

Perhaps those numbers are far too generous, but keep in mind, it's an estimate for just the *Milky Way* alone, so when we bring in the two trillion *other* galaxies in our known universe, even with the harshest conservative estimates, it's ludicrously unlikely that we're alone.

So, are we alone?

It's a question that has been asked discreetly by astronomers, philosophers, and wannabe teenage couples across history. In the context of alien life, it's perhaps the most poetic question ever asked—mostly since it leaves us dabbling on a subject we've got no direct evidence for.On one hand, there's a simple and obvious answer: maybe we're literally, sincerely alone in the universe. Maybe we've atrociously overestimated how common life is. Perhaps planets like Earth are so awesomely rare that intelligence hasn't popped up anywhere else in our corner of the universe.

This notion, dubbed the *Rare Earth* hypothesis, isn't worth ignoring. In 1984, astronomer Fred Hoyle suggested the odds of one single-celled organism tossing itself together in an ocean is about 1-in-$10^{40,000}$ for any given planet. Those aren't odds you'd want to bet your money on. It would take a full twenty pages of zeroes just to jot that probability down, and since my publisher still withholds the page limit, we won't be doing that.

WHAT A BEAUTIFUL DAY IN THE NEIGHBOURHOOD

By those standards, Earth is a winner in a near-impossible cosmic lottery.

We shouldn't be *surprised* to exist—based on the latest theories, our universe is probably infinite in size, which gives it an infinite supply of planets, and thus infinitely many shots at the cosmic lottery, more than enough to win infinitely many times. But Hoyle's estimate goes to explain why we don't see any other civilizations in *our own* galaxy. If everyone in the world bought lottery tickets, you wouldn't expect to find two winners in the exact same neighbourhood. Our closest cosmic neighbours might be trillions of light-years away, far outside our little observable universe, likely babbling about how odd it is that nobody's contacted them either.

On the other hand, the dubious answer to the Fermi Paradox is that clever, intelligent life is *common* in our isolated block of the universe, but it's got this unfortunate habit of blowing itself to smithereens before it ever has the chance to explore the universe. Maybe something goes wrong, planet after planet, that just *stops* alien societies from advancing into space.

Is total bombs-in-your-face annihilation a universal checkpoint across all life? This book isn't meant to be that bleak—although let's be honest, if you were looking for butterflies and rainbows, you made a questionable choice at the bookstore—but it's worth a reckoning: if such an absurd number of freak-accidents and flukes in the *past* have led to our existence *now*, what shot have we got at the future?

Setting Sail

From the perspective of a teenage writer, all people expect our age group to be doing is breaking boundaries. But take a look at recent human development, and you'll see this whole "boundary-breaking" thing isn't just a teenage habit; our whole species has been doing it for ages.

Back in the greyscale days of 1903, airplanes were a fanciful idea that seemed plausible on paper but crashed in practice. For the October 9th editorial of the *New York Times*, a column took a stab at the budding science of aviation. Two days earlier, the aviator Samuel Langley had crashed his prototype airplane, egging the newspaper to write that a flying plane might become a feasible project in the next "one million to ten million years."

Sixty-nine days later—a tad bit sooner than predicted—the two Wright brothers, Wilbur and Orville, flew their aircraft into the sky at Kitty Hawk. Almost overnight, we broke into the open skies—a realm that had been reserved to myths and folklore for centuries.

Fast-forward to 1926, and the rocketeer Robert Goddard fired up the first liquid-fuelled rocket in the world—a two-foot canister which fizzled out about 12 metres in the air. The world's first satellite, *Sputnik I*, rode atop a liquid-fuelled booster rocket just 31 years later—and a dozen years past that, liquid-fuelled rockets were landing humans on the surface of the Moon. We found a method to toss ourselves off the planet that raised us—another place that, for centuries, had been a figment of our legends and imaginations.

Bombshell invention after bombshell invention has rocked our species over the ages. The disease of smallpox, once a reaper of society that claimed over 30% of the lives it infected, was completely eradicated by 1980 thanks to global vaccination efforts. Our global life expectancy more than doubled in a century, from 32 to over 70 years. The internet went public in 1991, and a fleeting decade later, mobile phones squeezed more knowledge into your typical pant pocket than the Library of Alexandria ever held in its thousand-year-long history.

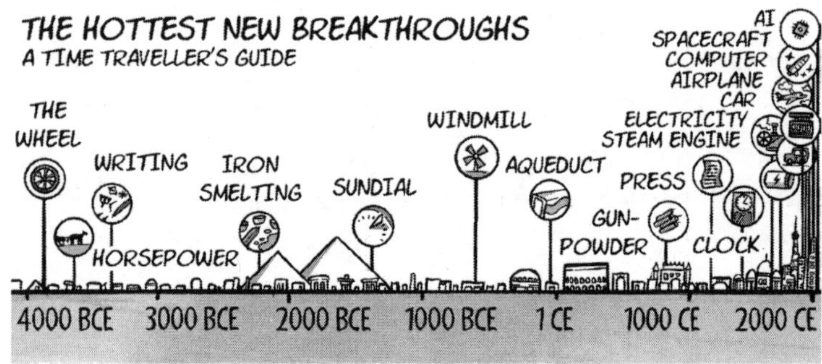

If alien surveyors had inspected our world, they might've assumed we were on track to settle the entire galaxy if they ignored the fact that, in the same century, we *also* came close to burning off the ozone layer, choking our skies with CO_2 greenhouse gases, and dynamiting our civilization in a nuclear tempest. The superpowers of the world haven't exactly tended gently.

To give a bite-size montage of our follies, between the 1930s and 1960s, the industries of our planet tossed chemicals known as chlorofluorocarbons (or CFCs if you're short on time) into the atmosphere; we made a killing on fridges and hairsprays with CFCs as their main ingredient. We *also* made a literal killing off the ozone layer, in the sense that these CFCs left a gaping hole in our bulletproof sunshield over Antarctica, letting volatile solar radiation down to the surface.

Two decades later, in the hellbent frenzy of the Cold War's nuclear arms race, our species crafted nukes into the 1980s until almost 70,000 warheads sat upon the push of a button—enough to snuff out all of human civilization itself. Twenty-eight nuclear wars *almost* erupted in the 20th Century—and of course, since you're still reading these words, none actually did.

Back in 1979, one faulty computer chip notified US president Jimmy Carter that 1,400 Soviet missiles had been recklessly blasted at the United States, demanding an instant retaliation. Eighteen B-52 nuclear bomber aircraft were locked and loaded for takeoff by the time the mission was scrubbed as a false alarm. Honestly, if you thought that typo on *your* text message was bad, trust me, you're fine.

Self-defence has been a popular go-to solution, and it's old news; your ancestors were the people who ran away from lions or hunted them for meat. Those individuals who've attempted to befriend and get amicable with lions are probably not the ancestors of anyone.

But it's worth mentioning some good news: we're still here!

With Earth's ozone layer in serious peril, the United Nations convened in the *Montreal Protocol* of 1987, which resulted in the banning of CFCs in 2010 and seeing their usage drop to practically nothing. Our sunshield of ozone is set to recover by 2040 if we're steadfast in our efforts. As for the nukes, the USA and USSR signed the *Intermediate-Range Nuclear Forces Treaty* in 1987, slowly dismantling their nuclear gadgetry—and the world has deactivated 85% of them since. Our effort isn't a sell-out success story yet, but it's not a box office bomb either.

In 2023, for the first time in history, our species invested more money on solar power than oil. At the 2019 UN Climate Summit, it was made clear that 70% of our carbon emissions could be axed with technology we've *already* got in our pockets. For the young readers out there, we'll be alive to determine whether our blue world passes Fermi's Paradox or fails it—and have a voice in which direction Earth leans. We could make landfall on over a dozen worlds before the end of this century, but what'll inspire the leaders of our world to tend to *this* planet's future? I'll be brutally honest: it's astronomy.

And yes, if you've tasted the theme of this book, I might be *a little* biased. But ever since nations began flinging astronauts above the atmosphere, they've returned with a deeply changed feeling about the Earth as a whole; they experience the iconic "Pale Blue Dot" shoved in front of their faces, sometimes for months at a time.

It's a reaction known as the *overview effect*. Apollo 9 astronaut Russell Schweikart once said, "When you go around the Earth in an hour and a half, you begin to recognize that your identity is with the whole thing."

It's a bird's-eye view that words hardly do justice. Of course, a commercial ticket to the International Space Station robs your wallet of about $60 million, reserving the overview effect to a select few seasoned astronauts and space-fanatic billionaires. But it doesn't have to be.

Looking at the stats, we're a species who's ludicrously outspoken against war, but can't ever seem to prepare for it hard enough. Despite the UN's 2017 *Treaty on the Prohibition of Nuclear Weapons*, our civilization still tossed $125 billion into nuclear weapons technology in 2023, along with $3.35 *trillion* into developing armed weapons. It makes rockets look dirt-cheap; it costs just $192 million to launch a four-seater *Dragon* spacecraft on a *Falcon 9* rocket.

So with a little persuasion, it'd cost $9.4 billion to launch the leaders of the world's 195 nations on a short jet-fuelled jaunt above the atmosphere, for them to witness, with their own eyes, the tender planet they're leading.

For a bonus $890 billion, we could launch into space each of the ~18,500 active military commanders and generals in the world—all for less than 28% of our planet's war budget in 2023. Would the world take a different stance on war, the climate, and human welfare if our admirals prime ministers, and presidents could really see just how unimaginably fragile the Earth is? Imagine a policy that decreed our leaders get an all-expenses-paid trip on a rocket, not for the sake of promoting any political agendas, but just to *look* at Earth. Just to catch a glimpse of the overview effect.

Until then, we ground-dwelling earthlings can only share words and imagine.

That's one of the reasons I feel astronomy is so essential in our world. Sure, it's not a field that will drop any practical life advice at family dinners—it's a subject that often garners the hallmark "when will we ever need to know this!?" response from kids—but it's more than just a mishmash of facts; it's a way of seeing the world. It's a perspective that no other vantage point can offer. It's like a set of eyes for our entire civilization, and only recently—a century back at most—has humanity really begun to see.

In 1995, at the *Observatoire de Haute-Provence* in France, a planet named *51 Pegasi b* was glimpsed outside our solar system; it was the first of 5,765 worlds that we've spotted across the galaxy—and honestly, by the time this book goes to print, there's almost guaranteed to be more. How many chances for life to take hold a second time? How many unfathomable histories playing out across the universe right now, each as mind-meltingly vast as our own?

We already know, from at least one planet—our Earth—that flapping wings evolved four separate times, echolocation twice, a nervous system likely twice, green photosynthesis 62 times, and eyes perhaps 65 times. If a single one of those distant plants spawned life, it might not be so estranged from us after all.

In June 2019, less than a second ago on our galactic timeline, a small book-sized satellite spread its wings while in orbit around the Earth. This spacecraft, CalTech's *Lightsail II* satellite, deployed a 32-square-metre sail to catch the tailwinds of sunshine itself, using sunlight as its propulsion drive—no fuel, no rockets, nothing but light.

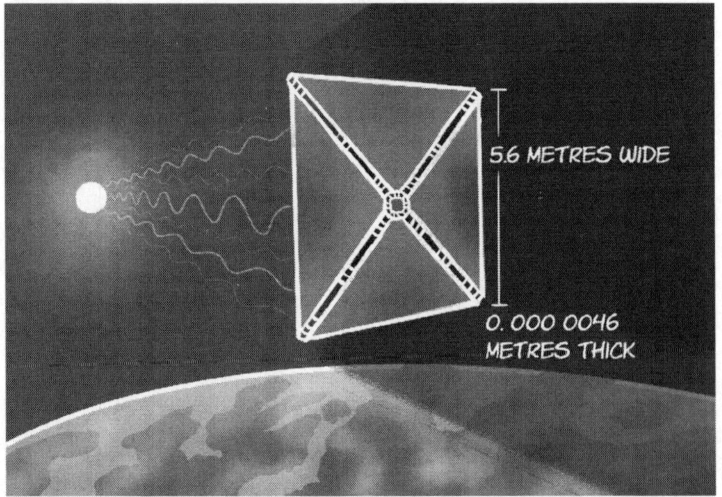

Ever since the 1860s, thanks to the work of physicist James Clerk Maxwell, we've known that beams of light could kick some thrust on an object—and with a big enough sail, Carl Sagan envisioned in the 1970s that starships might one day be lofted on the Sun's rays.

With *Lightsail II*, that vision came alive; its solar sail carried it over 3,000 metres higher in its orbit. It was a ridiculously basic ship compared to what we'll surely be using a millennium down the road, but still, it was our first real attempt at spooning across the cosmic ocean.

This was our inaugural solar-sailing cruise. Many chapters down the line, those solar sails might waft our descendants across the galaxy, but that's a tale for generations hence.

Having evolved quite a bit since the Twenty-first Century, those descendants might look back to the olden days of a distant planet known as Earth and remember us—a species who resembled them in almost every way. They'll remember how, just this century, we sailed into the universe—a feat that those descendants might take for granted as much as we take a ferry trip to Crete as pretty ordinary.

And you, reading these words, are alive to witness that sail unfolding.

For the first time, we realized the precarity of Earth's environment and reconciled it; we learned to trust each other across our borders—both geographical and genetic—and at long last, we recognized that in lieu of the baffling amount we had in common, it was probably in our best interests *not* to shoot one another based on 0.08% of a genome's difference. We all agreed it was best to leave that level of nitpicking to accountants.

Hopefully, as our solar system crosses its 20th galactic birthday and as future historians map the next galactic minute of our *own* history, our pages will keep taking turns for the better. As a tribute to the 110 billion humans

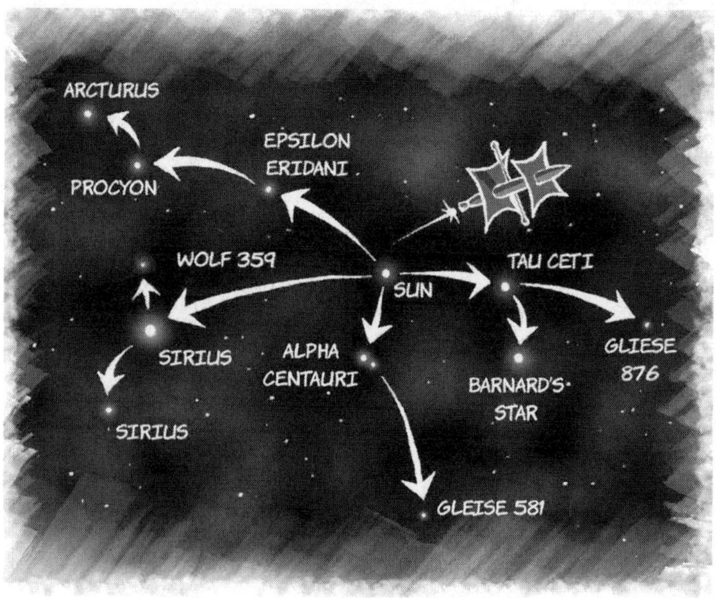

who've lived and loved and died on this planet to raise everything here today, let's not lose sight of our place in the universe. There's a magnificent possible future ahead of us.

We're the latest movement of an ongoing symphony of atoms, orchestrated by the laws of physics, that's been composing over five trillion days. We exist thanks to a complete annihilation of most of the universe, a dance of dark matter, an enormous black hole collapsing, the explosion of a distant star, a head-on smack up from an entire planet, an asteroid hailstorm, a union of three chemical ingredients against astounding odds, a series of gene-altering viruses, one partnership between two cells, a total recycling of our atmosphere, a planet-shackling meteorite impact, a few galactic rollercoaster rides through a radiation beam, and a sheer curiosity driving us forward.

But sure, go ahead and call your Monday mornings boring.

Time: An Epilogue

It's taken 13.8 billion years for entropy to sauté humanity into existence, and it certainly won't hold its beer for us; it'll saunter onward, mixing and mincing the universe into a messier and messier state, brushing right past our unmarked chapter of the cosmic history. So, with such a grandiose plan for the future of humanity, how high should we hold our hopes? Let's take one last look through time, in the other direction. It's not exactly a fairytale Hollywood ending, It's not exactly a fairytale Hollywood ending, but our cosmic future offers some serious solace for the present but our cosmic future offers some solace for the present times.

If there's any decent way to begin this not-so-Hollywood conclusion, it's the future of our human genome. Unless we make a bombshell breakthrough on immortality in the next century, it goes without saying that within the next thirteen galactic seconds—about 100 years—almost all the folks who are currently alive today will be dead. Of course, that's just flesh and bones; for the genetic aspect, close to 99.9% of their traits survive in the cells of anyone who's descended from them. Dial the clocks ahead 3,400 years—seven galactic minutes—and you're either an ancestor to no one, or to *everyone* alive in that distant age. You might *be* that distant relic connecting the future family trees of all humans in 5400 CE, though they'll have no clue.

If we *really* skip ahead, the flora and fauna that decorate our landscapes begin to change. It's no surprise that Earth—the blue beacon of life—is also the biggest killing machine in the universe. Even in the absence of people crate-digging the ecosystem, the Earth still naturally snipes out 0.01% of its living species every century. This means, if we speedrun 4.6 million years into the future, less than 1% of today's species are still around. Forests are flocked with new insects and birds, the seas hold their own new beasts, and humans, if we give ourselves a little optimism, could be among that 1% who are still around. But stretch the clocks further, and even our planets begin to change.

In 50 million years, Mars is dealt its own serious smack as its nearest moon, the potato-shaped Phobos, plunges down in a doomed inward spiral until it collides. On Earth, at around the same time, Africa's large tectonic plate collides with Europe, sealing off the Mediterranean Sea, thus ending Britain's fifty-million-year shipping route via the Suez Canal. The British are forced to reroute via the South Atlantic, or colonize the Milky Way galaxy—a task that could be feasable in as little as a million years.

Halfway to our next galactic birthday—100 million Earth years from now—our planet has at last finished replacing the fossil fuels we've drilled and scooped out in the last century alone, erasing the last inkling of evidence that modern humans ever touched the Earth at all.

At this point in the future, not a smidge of our modern society is left. The 21st Century is an obscure corner of our history, riddled with stories and electronic files, but physically reduced to a two-millimetre-thick band of slightly radioactive rock buried underneath a kilometre of solid sediment layers. Everyone who's alive today is bound to become part of that layer, homogenized into atoms. Our stain lies just slightly above the rust that was etched by cyanobacteria in the rock museums of our planet's history.

One galactic birthday—225 million Earth years into our future—and the continents of Africa, Europe and Asia are beginning their plunge into North and South America. The tectonic plates, atop which we're all captive, writhe around our planet's surface. At this point, the Atlantic Ocean closes off, forcing the world's landmasses into one group hug supercontinent known as *Pangaea Ultima*, shunning the oceans onto their own half of the world. As collateral damage, the British economy is once again forced to swap its shipping routes, likely opting for galactic colonization.

Two galactic birthdays—550 million years—ahead on our timeline, the Sun is sizzling about 6% brighter than it does nowadays, and that's more than enough to start simmering down our planet's oceans like an overcooked stir-fry soup. As the seafloor slowly dries up like a sunbaked raisin, plate tectonics grind to a halt, which effectively quells all geologic events.

Volcanoes no longer belch CO_2 into our skies, and all plants—tailored to *breathe* CO_2 by four billion years of evolution, start to suffocate on their own planet. Having less plants means less oxygen, and less ozone to shield the Earth from the Sun's ultraviolet bullets. In a mass extinction that would be almost sardonic if it weren't, well, a *mass extinction* event, it happens that carbon dioxide—the gas that we protested and engineered our society to *remove* from our skies—is precisely what kills the Earth, not in its abundance, but its absence.

Three galactic birthdays—750 million Earth years—into the future, the Earth's poles become the best vacation sites on the planet, kissed with temperatures hot enough for palm trees to thrive. The equator has probably been scalded to a barren desert; Antarctica has morphed into a tropical paradise that paints the base of our brownish-blue planet a vibrant green.

Five galactic birthdays—1.1 billion years ahead—the Sun has quashed almost all of Earth's living systems. The plants, starved of carbon dioxide, have withered away, collapsing the entire food chain. That lack of oxygen undresses the Earth of its ozone layer, lasering the surface in ultraviolet rays that scramble life's genes.

Antarctica has cooked to a balmy 50°C, pushing it outside the five-star Airbnb range and into the less-desirable desert hellscape that it soon becomes. The oceans begin to bubble up into a planet-coating cloud of vapour. By the time the calendar strikes 1.3 billion years, the era of complex life—kickstarted way back in the Cambrian—bids us a fond farewell. Earth goes back to being a planet ruled by bacteria, same as it was for most of its history. Flagella are, once again, the most advanced ways of getting around.

Our future timer hits 1.6 billion years; Earth has swivelled around the Milky Way galaxy seven times since the long-forsaken 21st Century. The last cell on our heat-scorched planet—a fellow I might call our "Last Universal Common Descendant," one last lump of stardust fighting against entropy—sizzles to a crisp by the lakeside of an evaporating pond in Antarctica. The era of life on Earth comes to a wrap. The oceans completely boil away to nothing. The British are forced to abandon the notion of shipping altogether.

Except it's not over so soon. Earth probably won't be the last world our descendants visit, since back in the 21st Century, one of its species discovered its knack for world-hopping—and if we give that species a little optimism, chances are they'll be capable of fleeing to abodes on far-off worlds before Earth cooks them. That final dying cell might not be the end of Earth life at all; *we'll* be carrying that torch across the universe. At about the same time Earth loses its livelihood, Mars inherits it.

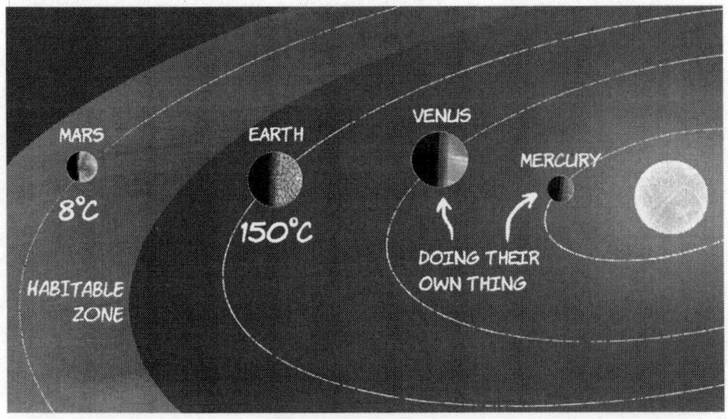

At this point, 1.6 billion years into the future, the Sun strikes our solar system with 16% more light and energy, causing its habitable zone—that sacred distance where water trickles as a liquid—to grow snugly into the orbit of the Red Planet, thawing its ice-stricken landscape. Mars is flushed into a lush, temperate planet, about 8°C worldwide, perhaps laying the foundation for a new chapter of life's history—a Martian chapter lasting over three billion years.

The clock strikes two billion years. The Milky Way has twirled nine times since the 21st Century, and over that immense timespan, our galaxy's gravity has tugged on its close neighbour, the Andromeda galaxy, so much that they're starting to collide.

In a billion-year-long acrobatics show, the two galaxies punch through each other, tossing trillions of stars into deep space, setting off a cosmic fireworks display as gas clouds get rammed into one another. Billions of new solar systems are born, beginning their *own* outrageous stories as ours burns to a charcoaled cinder. That fireworks show, at least for the audience of Earth, will have a crowd of zero.

The clock hits 3.5 billion years; Earth is now glowing a faint red as its surface screams at an unrentable 1,100°C. Our atmosphere is choked with steam as what used to be the oceans, all 1.3 billion km^3 of them, fill the skies with vapour.

As a slight plus, the whole Milky-Way-Andromeda galactic fiasco settles down; the two galaxies merge into one massive glob of stars that astronomers have so creatively named Milkdromeda. The Earth's galactic citizenship changes.

Five billion years into our future, 22 galactic birthdays away, the Moon has drifted so far from Earth that it's no longer tethered by our planet's gravity; in its own wild looping orbit, the Moon becomes a quasi-planet, and so in this distant era, we're at last forced to rename it. Around the same time, Mars heats up to room-temperature. Jupiter's moons begin to thaw.

Six billion years ahead; the Sun cracks and fizzles its last spurts of hydrogen, which smothers its core in carbon ash. The Sun's burning squall of nuclear fusion begins to explode on overdrive mode, pushing outward and bloating the Sun to over 250 times its current size. It grows so enormous that Mercury, Venus, and Earth now orbit *inside* it. We can infer, with a rather simplistic logical leap, that a planet orbiting inside a star is a planet no more.

The Earth is vaporized, obliterated down to atoms, and absorbed into the very star that birthed it.

Our long-forgotten human fossils get charred up into a hot plasma of protons and neutrons, which basically barbecues us back into the stellar mist of subatomic particles we used to be before humanity, or the Earth, ever existed.

Now, humans being humans, we're probably either extinct or dillydallying out among the galaxies by this point, so either way, the Sun's death throes aren't a huge concern for us.

Eight billion years ahead: Jupiter's icy moon Europa has likely melted into one huge planet-sized ocean, holding more water than Earth ever did in its eleven-billion-year lifespan. If anything evolves on that distant blue dot, it's living on borrowed time; the languishing Sun soon coughs off its outer layers and smolders into a sullen white dwarf star. Everything in the solar system freezes.

But even here, about 660 galactic years in the future, our universe has barely begun.

Across the next 100 billion years of our history, our local neighbourhood of galaxies, the so-called Local Group (although "local" is a meaningless term in astronomy, with those galaxies being over 100 quintillion kilometres away) begins to merge into one single galaxy in a pirouette of galactic mayhem. That galaxy holds over a trillion stars, giving life another trillion-or-so chances to evolve from scratch. Our galactic citizenship changes yet again.

About 660 galactic years in the future—150 billion Earth years, if it even matters now that Earth no longer exists—our cosmos has ballooned to such a ridiculously huge scale that we won't be able to see those galaxies anymore.

Space has always been expanding, but now, by this point, it's inflated so much that all the other galaxies have been dragged outside the visible horizon of our universe, hiding them away forever. But the stars keep shining; our universe, even here, has ticked across just 0.2% of its starlit shelf life. This means, with the sheer numbers, that 99.8% of our universe's star-studded history will be spent in complete galactic isolation—and we humans are alive in that one *sliver* of an era where the universe *isn't*.

It's quite a privilege, here in the 21st Century, to be able to point our telescopes at the sky and have two trillion galaxies in front of our eyes. Most of the creatures who'll *ever* exist in this universe will see *one* galaxy only—their own—and have no clue the cosmos was ever larger than that alone.

In a trillion years, 4,500 galactic years down the road, the faint light of the Cosmic Microwave Background radiation withers down until it's lost forever in the obscure crackling static buzz of ordinary space. If any clues about the Big Bang are still lingering on, it'll be thanks to the research done by creatures alive in the lustrous age of the cosmos where it *was* visible—the era we're currently living in. With those sheer numbers again, about 99% of our universe's stars will shine in a cosmos that's devoid of the light of the Big Bang, erasing that history forever for any clever critters who might live around those stars. Yet here we humans are, with that cosmic light still detectable, clear as day, at night. Turn on your radio, detune it, listen to the ear-splitting static, and hear it: the crackle of the Big Bang's light, at least 1% of it, weaving through your room at this very moment.

Looking even further, we have to ask ourselves: how long can life exist in a universe that's unavoidably being tossed into a stew of chaos and disorder at the whims of entropy? In less than 10 trillion years, the stars begin to wilt—first the bright blue ones, then the modest yellow, and lastly the faintest red dwarfs. Eventually, their stellar gas clouds become strewn apart, starving them of hydrogen fuel. Like seeds growing in spent soil, nothing new sprouts. The most ancient stars finally snuff out after 100 trillion years, freezing every last planet. For all we know, life needs an energy source, and without stars, the show's over. Over timespans so tedious it makes even morning lectures feel like an eyeblink, over something like 10^{43} years, our protons fall apart and decay into a thin cloud of subatomic particles and antiparticles—a haunting mirror image of the moment right after the Big Bang itself. And then darkness.

It can't be stressed enough: our time here is fleeting. I'll bid you to burn it well.

A hundred *trillion* years—that's life's entire chapter in our cosmic story. Our universe isn't currently looking a day over 13.8 *billion* years old, so we're not even 0.014%

of the way through that life-infested chapter of the cosmos. If this book's entire length represented those 100 trillion years, our universe's current age would sum up to these five words in bold.

Now grab the period at the end of that sentence. Cut it into a thousand pieces. Pick up one of its fragments. That's human history. Slice that fragment into a thousand pieces again; collect a mote of that dust. That's a human lifespan. That's you and I on our cosmic timeline.

So that's our last little reckoning—one last thing we all share in common: a little blip of cosmic time to spend here on Earth. It's all too easy to lose ourselves in grandiose visions of a future we imagine lasts forever. But maybe, in the face of that timeline, a few more of us can make peace with Now. If the mind-mashing size of cosmic history has anything to teach us, it's not to bother dwelling on that mortally stupid thing you uttered to your high school crush back in twelfth grade, or that senseless comment someone made about you. In a cosmic eyeblink from now, we'll all be a sparse cloud of atoms floating in the void anyways.

So, what about Now? Seems like a perfect place to wrap this up.

At this moment, there are 8.7 million species on Earth. One of those is humanity, comprised of 8.2 billion people. There's a common sentiment—almost a meme, in fact—in the astronomy community that says something along these lines: Earth is farcically insignificant, we couldn't matter less, and one day this whole human fiasco will daftly crumble to dust. Sound at all familiar? Even speaking for die-hard astronomers, I'd beg to differ.

Yes, we're on a flea-sized pebble zipping around a pinprick of starlight in an ordinary galaxy of 200 billion suns, in a colossal ocean of two trillion galaxies, in a universe that might be even larger. But across all those galaxies, stars, and planets, only one world is unequivocally, hands-down, one-hundred-percent known to harbour life. And we're living on it.

Yes, there's something like 10 septillion planets in the known universe—each with their own beaches and shores, lightning storms, eclipses, vast canyons, mountains and skies—but for all we know, those worlds are being witnessed by no one. Quadrillions of sunsets go unseen, crashing waves unheard, and rocky hills untouched. Except here.

Until SETI lands a jackpot, Earth is the only place in the known universe where *anything* is really appreciated *at all.* Around us, we've got dark matter to ponder and Dark Matter to drink, whether we're raising a glass in the air, or a telescope to the sky.

Being alive in this universe is just about the most baffling lottery win we could imagine. To really hammer down that point, I'll leave you with some numbers.

There's been something like ten duodecillion (10^{40}) creatures who've lived and died across our planet's whole history, and almost all of them were single-celled blobs. From a 1999 North Carolina study, it takes something like 250 letters of DNA, at the bare minimum, to set off the chemical tapestry needed to run a basic functioning cell.

Now take humans, who've got 3.1 *billion* letters of DNA in our genetic databanks.

And now take the small ruffled flower of *Paris japonica*, a plant that, in 2024, was found to have 150 *billion* nucleotide letters of DNA crammed into its cells—the longest known genome on Earth, eclipsing ours by almost 50 times. Life is a random card shuffle of genetic code, and we're somewhere on the vast continuum of all its possible jumbles.

As those genetic cards get shuffled each new generation, mistakes and mix-ups are routine show business in the DNA-copying factories inside each cell. Thanks to those mix-ups, sometimes life evolves flippers; other times it's feet. Sometimes it's tails, or claws, or flagella. Sometimes it sprouts leaves, other times it grows fur. Sometimes it's single-celled, other times it's a colony of trillions. Sometimes it's brown hair, sometimes blonde, or somewhere in between. With every error, a new genome is born—a new, unique way of being alive.

We can label and group up creatures who look similar, but the truth is, no two living critters have ever shared a perfect photocopied genome their entire lives. Genomes are too tender, too fettered by random errors, to make perfect copies. Of all the 10^{40} different creatures of Earth's history, none of them were identical.

There's such a mind-boggling number of ways to slice and dice a genome: with over 150 billion letters to shuffle up, and a menagerie of about 100,000 different genes to edit, nature has a theoretical palette spanning over $10^{90,000,000,000}$ possible creatures based on DNA alone.

This number is so ineffably huge that I'm not in any good position to put it in perspective without imploding my 3.1-pound human brain. Even if life were brewing at full throttle on every planet and moon in the observable universe, starting at the Big Bang and ending after 100 trillion years after the last star smoulders to atomic ash, just about 10^{68} living beings would come to be. That doesn't even *dent* the roster of $10^{90,000,000,000}$ theoretical unique organisms. There's simply not enough time, in the entire lifespan of our universe, to evolve all possible living critters.

Keep in mind, that's just *DNA alone*—a tiny molecule that scientists at the Tokyo Institute of Technology have already theorized over 1,160,000 possible chemical alternatives for. There's a hauntingly vast number of ways life can exist—and our planet has evolved so, so few of them. If our whole cosmos represented every possible life, nature has evolved much less than an atom's worth. And yet, here we are.

From the unimaginable mishmash of genetic combos, you and I are just two editions. But we're two editions among the preposterously small sliver of creatures who'll ever get to exist *at all* in this universe. Against such stupendous odds, we get to actually *experience* the story of the universe firsthand. Maybe there are other lives out there; someday we might meet them. But until then, we get to continue on this 13.8-billion-year-long tale of atoms that one day became aware, looked around, and realized their cosmos existed.

I'll raise a glass to that.

Acknowledgements

Writing a book across billions of years, in a fitting manner, ate up a huge amount of time. I'm grateful, first and foremost, for my parents and their unwavering support, and for allowing me to leech off their groceries like an ingrown home parasite. You birthed me—already a huge plus for my livelihood—and have nurtured my love of the cosmos ever since; you'll always be the stars at the center of my universe. Huge thanks to my sister—and I *wasn't* coerced into thanking her here—for allowing me to utilize her iPad to sketch my artwork. Sincerely and honestly, my life would be far too dull without you.

I'm indebted to the Nerd Cult of Mount Douglas Secondary School and its beloved Challenge Program—the finest army of geeks anyone could ever wish for—and the leaders of this academic cult, my teachers Neal Johnson and Ted Meldrum. Thank you for your support; thank you for being flexible as this book's research devoured my study hours faster than you devoured my GPA. For chatting with me about Dark Matter (the beer), I'd like to thank Sean Hoyne from the Hoyne Brewing Company.

For chatting with me about dark matter (the cosmic subject) and countless other scientific inquiries, I'd like to thank Dr. Aleksa Alaica (University of British Columbia, Anthropology), Dr. Darlene Weston (University of British Columbia, Anthropology), Dr. Georgia G. Soares (Penn State University, Geosciences), Simon Smith (University of Victoria, Astronomy), Dr. Marc Kamionkowski (John Hopkins University, Physics and Astronomy), and Dr. Dorothy H. Paul (Ret. University of Victoria, Biology) for sprinkling your esteemed knowledge and resources over this book's development.

Of course, this all would have amounted to nothing more than a tatty Microsoft Word document without the spellbinding book-binding magic enacted by the incredible team at Linda Leith Publishing. A million thanks to Linda Leith, editors Leila Marshy, Kaiya Smith Blackburn, Jennifer McMorran, Edward He, Christina Soubassakou, and Shakiya Williams, and designer Debbie Geltner.

I'd like to express my gratitude to the astronomers who've inspired me; thank you to Dr. Jon Willis and Dr. Julio Navarro (University of Victoria, Physics and Astronomy), Dr. Lisa Kaltenegger (Cornell University, Astrobiology), and the astronomer-poet-visionary Carl Sagan. Closer to home, I'm forever thankful for the RASCals at the Royal Astronomical Society of Canada Victoria Centre, whose support, passion, and opportunities have truly changed my life. Your encouragement at the Dominion Astrophysical Observatory and *SkyNews* magazine has meant so much. You folks mean the universe to me.

To round it off, in the spirit of *Cosmic Wonder*, I'd like to give a shoutout to Hypatia of Alexandria, Giordano Bruno, Galileo Galilei, Svante Arrhenius, Mikhail Budyko, Andrei Linde, James Clerk Maxwell, Ole Rømer, Jocelyn Bell Burnell, Frank Drake, Enrico Fermi, Alexei Sharov, Jane Goodall, and everyone who's left their mark on our vast understanding of this beautiful universe. Seriously, I couldn't have written this book without y'all.

References

Aaij, R. et al. "Measurement of CP Violation in the Decay B+→K+π0." *Physical Review Letters* 126, no. 9 (March 2021). https://doi.org/10.1103/physrevlett.126.091802.

Anslow, L. "In 1903, New York Times Predicted That Airplanes Would Take 10 million Years to Develop." Big Think. October 18, 2023. https://bigthink.com/pessimists-archive/air-space-flight-impossible/.

Ascher, M. *Ethnomathematics: A Multicultural View of Mathematical Ideas*. Oxford: Routledge, 1994).

Avila, G. et. al. "Role of TGF-β on Cardiac Structural and Electrical Remodeling." *Vascular Health and Risk Management* 4, no. 6 (December 2008): 1289–1300. https://doi.org/10.2147/vhrm.s3985.

Bailey, D. H. et. al. "The quest for PI." *The Mathematical Intelligencer* 19, no. 1 (December 1997): 50–56. https://doi.org/10.1007/bf03024340.

Barragán, O. et al. "K2-141 b." *Astronomy and Astrophysics* 612 (May 2018). https://doi.org/10.1051/0004-6361/201732217

Baum, B. et al. "On the Origin of the Nucleus: A Hypothesis." *Microbiology and Molecular Biology Reviews* 87, no. 4 (November 2023). https://doi.org/10.1128/mmbr.00186-21.

Bennett, C. L. et. al. "Nine-Year Wilkinson Microwave Anisotropy Probe (WMAP) Observations: Final Maps and Results." *The Astrophysical Journal Supplement Series* 208, no. 2 (September 2013). https://doi.org/10.1088/0067-0049/208/2/20.

Bennetzen, J. L., & Ma, J. "The Genetic Colinearity of Rice and Other Cereals on the Basis of Genomic Sequence Analysis." *Current Opinion in Plant Biology* 6, no. 2 (April 2003): 128–133. https://doi.org/10.1016/s1369-5266(03)00015-3.

Benowitz, A. "How Many Generals Are There in the US Military." Armorial Register. October 4, 2024. https://www.armorial-register.com/how-many-generals-are-in-us-military/.

Blätke, M., & Bräutigam, A. "Evolution of C4 Photosynthesis Predicted by Constraint-Based Modelling." *eLife* 8 (December 2019). https://doi.org/10.7554/elife.49305.

Bonocora, R. P., & Shub, D. A. "A Self-Splicing Group I Intron in DNA Polymerase Genes of T7-Like Bacteriophages." *Journal of Bacteriology* 186, no. 23 (December 2004): 8153–8155. https://doi.org/10.1128/jb.186.23.8153-8155.2004.

Bosmia, A. et. al. "Physician and Heretic Who Described the Pulmonary Circulation." *Journal of Cardiology* 167, no. 2 (July 2013): 318–321. https://doi.org/10.1016/j.ijcard.2012.06.046.

Bovy, J., & Tremaine, S. "On the Local Dark Matter Density." *The Astrophysical Journal* 756, no. 1 (August 2012): 89. https://doi.org/10.1088/0004-637x/756/1/89.

Broecker, F., & Moelling, K. "What Viruses Tell Us About Evolution and Immunity: Beyond Darwin?" *Annals of the New York Academy of Sciences* 1447, no. 1 (April 2019): 53–68. https://doi.org/10.1111/nyas.14097.

Brundrett, M. C. "Coevolution of Roots and Mycorrhizas of Land Plants." *New Phytologist* 154, no. 2 (April 2002): 275–304. https://doi.org/10.1046/j.1469-8137.2002.00397.x.

Budyko, M. I. "The Future Climate." *Eos* 53, no. 10 (October 1972): 868–874. https://doi.org/10.1029/eo053i010p00868.

Buniy, R. V., & Hsu, S. D. "Everything is entangled." *Physics Letters B* 718, no. 2 (December 2012): 233–236. https://doi.org/10.1016/j.physletb.2012.09.047.Burkhardt, P. et al. "Syncytial Nerve Net in a Ctenophore Adds Insights on the Evolution of Nervous Systems." *Science* 380, no. 6642 (April 2023): 293–297. https://doi.org/10.1126/science.ade5645.

Burnell, J. B. "Cosmic Search Vol. 1, No. 1." Cosmic Search Magazine. December 1977. http://www.bigear.org/vol1no1/burnell.htm.

Cafferty, B. J. et al. "Searching for Possible Ancestors of RNA: The Self-Assembly Hypothesis for the Origin of Proto-RNA." *Nucleic Acids and Molecular Biology* 35 (August 2018): 143–174. https://doi.org/10.1007/978-3-319-93584-3_5.

Catling, D. C., & Zahnle, K. J. "The Archean Atmosphere." *Science Advances* 6, no. 9 (February 2020). https://doi.org/10.1126/sciadv.aax1420.

Chang, JT. "Recent Common Ancestors of All Present-Day Individuals." *Advances in Applied Probability* 31, no. 4 (July 2016): 1002–1026. http://www.stat.yale.edu/~jtc5/papers/Ancestors.pdf.

Choi, C. "How Hot Were the Oceans When Life First Evolved?" Astrobiology at NASA. https://shorturl.at/x1ctG.

"Clean energy investment is extending its lead over fossil fuels, boosted by energy security strengths." International Energy Agency 50. May 25, 2023. https://www.iea.org/news/clean-energy-investment-is-extending- its-lead-over-fossil-fuels-boosted-by-energy-security-strengths.

Collins, R. F. *Chocolate: A Cultural Encyclopedia*. Santa Barbara: ABC-Clio, 2022.

"Comparing Chimp, Bonobo and Human DNA." American Museum of Natural History. https://shorturl.at/EouKc.

"Cuneiform tablet: record of rations of beer, bread, oil, and onions for messengers." The Metropolitan Museum of Art. https://www.metmuseum.org/art/collection/search/327069.

Crawford, E. "Arrthenius' 1896 Model of the Greenhouse Effect in Context." *Ambio* 26, no. 1 (February 1997). http://www.jstor.org/stable/4314543.

Crockford P.W. et al. "The geologic history of primary productivity." *Curr Biol* 6,33, no. 21 (November 2023): 4741–4750. doi: 10.1016/j.cub.2023.09.040.

Daeschler, E. B. et al. "A Devonian Tetrapod-Like Fish and the Evolution of the Tetrapod Body Plan." *Nature* 440, no. 7085 (April 2006): 757–763. https://doi.org/10.1038/nature04639.

Damerow, P. "Sumerian Beer: The Origins of Brewing Technology in Ancient Mesopotamia." CDLI. January 22, 2012. https://cdli.mpiwg-berlin.mpg.de/articles/cdlj/2012-2.

D'Angelo, G., & Podolak, M. "Capture and Evolution of Planetesimals in Circumjovian Disks." *The Astrophysical Journal* 806, no. 2 (April 2015): 203. https://doi.org/10.1088/0004-637x/806/2/203.

"Dark Matter." Hoyne Brewing Co. https://www.hoynebrewing.ca/beer/dark-matter/.

Deamer, D. "The Role of Lipid Membranes in Life's Origin." *Life* 7, no. 1 (January 2017): 5. https://doi.org/10.3390/life7010005.

DeSilva, J. et al. "Human Brains Have Shrunk: The Questions Are When and Why." *Frontiers in Ecology and Evolution* 11 (June 2023). https://doi.org/10.3389/fevo.2023.1191274.

Dilke, O. Mathematics and *M*easurement. Berkley: University of California Press, 1987, 46.

Dizon, E. Z., & Pawlik, A. F. "The lower Palaeolithic record in the Philippines." *Quaternary International* 223–224 (September 2010): 444–450. https://doi.org/10.1016/j.quaint.2009.10.002.

"Dr. Robert H. Goddard, American Rocketry Pioneer." NASA. https://www.nasa.gov/dr-robert-h-goddard-american-rocketry-pioneer/.

"Drake Equation." SETI Institute. May 23, 2024. https://www.seti.org/drake-equation-index.

Dumas, Y. "Annotated Cosmic Call Primer." Smithsonian Magazine. September 22, 2016. https://www.smithsonianmag.com/science-nature/annotated-cosmic-call-primer-180960566/.

Elahi, F. et al. "Charged B Mesogenesis." *Physical Review* 105, no. 5 (March 2022). https://doi.org/10.1103/physrevd.105.055024.

Elor, G. et al. "Baryogenesis and dark matter from B mesons." *Physical Review* 99, no. 3 (February 2019). https://doi.org/10.1103/physrevd.99.035031.

Émie, A. et al. "Microbiomes of Clownfish and their Symbiotic Host Anemone Before their First Physical Contact." *Microbiome* 9, no. 1 (May 2021). https://doi.org/10.1186/s40168-021-01058-1.

England, J. "Statistical Physics of Self-Replication." *J. Chem. Phys.* 139, no. 12 (September 2013): 121923–121923. https://doi.org/10.1063/1.4818538.

"Evolutionary leap from fins to legs was surprisingly simple." ScienceDaily. March 16, 2016. https://www.sciencedaily.com/releases/2016/03/160308090800.htm.

"False Warnings of Soviet Missile Attacks Put U.S. Forces on Alert in 1979-1980." *National Security Archive.* March 16, 2020. https://nsarchive.gwu.edu/briefing-book/nuclear-vault/2020-03-16/

false-warnings-soviet-missile-attacks-during-1979-80-led-alert-actions-us-strategic-forces.

Ferentinos, G. et al. Early Seafaring Activity in the Southern Ionian Islands, Mediterranean Sea." *Journal of Archaeological Science* 39, no. 7 (July 2012): 2167–2176. https://doi.org/10.1016/j.jas.2012.01.032.

Fernández, P. et al. "A 160 Gbp Fork Fern Genome Shatters Size Record for Eukaryotes." *iScience* 27, no. 6 (May 2024). https://www.ncbi.nlm.nih.gov/pmc/articles/PMC11270024/.

Fiegl, A. "A Brief History of Chocolate." Smithsonian Magazine. November 16, 2013. https://www.smithsonianmag.com/arts-culture/a-brief-history-of-chocolate-21860917/?no-ist.

"Fritz Zwicky: Underrecognized Astronomer." American Museum of Natural History. https://www.amnh.org/learn-teach/curriculum-collections/cosmic-horizons-book/fritz-zwicky.

Fukasawa, Y. "Ecological memory and relocation decisions in fungal mycelial networks: responses to quantity and location of new resources." *The ISME Journal* 14, no. 2 (February 2019): 380–388. https://doi.org/10.1038/s41396-019-0536-3.

"Galactic Ghosts: Gaia Uncovers Major Event in the Formation of the Milky Way." ESA Science & Technology. October 31, 2018. https://sci.esa.int/web/gaia/-/60892-galactic-ghosts-gaia-uncovers-major-event-in-the-formation-of-the-milky-way.

Gary, D. E. "Astronomy Lecture Number 26." NJIT. https://web.njit.edu/~gary/202/Lecture26.html.

Ghosh, T. et al. "A Retroviral Link to Vertebrate Myelination Through Retrotransposon-RNA-Mediated Control of Myelin Gene Expression." *Cell* 187, no. 4, (February 2024): 814–830. https://doi.org/10.1016/j.cell.2024.01.011.

"Giordano Bruno." Stanford Encyclopedia of Philosophy. March 12, 2024. https://plato.stanford.edu/entries/bruno/.

Gitschier, J. "All About Mitochondrial Eve: An Interview with Rebecca Cann." *PLoS Genetics* 6, no. 5 (May 2010). https://doi.org/10.1371/journal.pgen.1000959.

Global Wind Energy Council. "There Are Over 341,000 Wind Turbines on the Planet: Here's How Much of a Difference They're Actually Making." GWEC. September 11, 2017. https://shorturl.at/5D50S.

Goodall, J. "Essays on Science and Society: Learning from the Chimpanzees, A Message Humans Can Understand." *Science* 282, no. 5397 (December 1998): 2184–2185. https://doi.org/10.1126/science.282.5397.2184.

Gracia, A. et al. "Craniosynostosis in the Middle Pleistocene Human Cranium 14 From the Sima de los Huesos, Atapuerca, Spain." *Proceedings of the National Academy of Sciences* 106, no. 16 (April 2009): 6573–6578. https://doi.org/10.1073/pnas.0900965106.

Gray, M. W. "Mitochondrial Evolution." *Cold Spring Harbor Perspectives in Biology* 4, no. 9 (2012). https://doi.org/10.1101/cshperspect.a011403.

Grosberg, R. K., & Strathmann, R. R. "The Evolution of Multicellularity: A Minor Major Transition?" *Annual Review of Ecology Evolution and Systematics* 38, no. 1 (December 2007): 621–654. https://doi.org/10.1146/annurev.ecolsys.36.102403.114735.

Guterres, A. "Remarks at 2019 Climate Action Summit." United Nations Secretary-General. September 23, 2019. https://www.un.org/sg/en/content/sg/speeches/2019-09-23/remarks-2019-climate-action-summit.

Hay, C. W., & Docherty, K. "Comparative Analysis of Insulin Gene Promoters." *Diabetes* 55, no. 12 (December 2006): 3201–3213. https://doi.org/10.2337/db06-0788.

Hayashida, F. M. "Ancient Beer and Modern Brewers: Ethnoarchaeological Observations of Chicha Production in Two Regions of the North Coast of Peru." *Journal of Anthropological Archaeology* 27, no. 2 (June 2008): 161–174. https://doi.org/10.1016/j.jaa.2008.03.003.

Hehenberger, E. et al. "Evidence for the Retention of Two Evolutionary Distinct Plastids in Dinoflagellates with Diatom Endosymbionts." *Genome Biology and Evolution* 6, no. 9 (September 2014): 2321–2334. https://doi.org/10.1093/gbe/evu182.

Heller, R. et al. "Habitability of the Early Earth: Liquid Water Under a Faint Young Sun Facilitated by Strong Tidal Heating Due to a Closer Moon." *PalZ* 95, no. 4 (November 2021): 563–575. https://doi.org/10.1007/s12542-021-00582-7.

Hellwig, H. et al. "Measurement of the Unperturbed Hydrogen Hyperfine Transition Frequency." *IEEE Transactions on Instrumentation and Measurement* 19, no. 4 (1970): 200–209. https://doi.org/10.1109/tim.1970.4313902.

Henderson J. C. et al. "One Among Millions: The Chemical Space of Nucleic Acid-Like Molecules." *Journal of Chemical Information and Modeling* 59, no. 10 (September 2019): 4266 DOI: 10.1021/acs.jcim.9b00632.

Herdman, M. et al. "Genome Size of Cyanobacteria." *Journal of General Microbiology* 111, no. 1 (March 1979): 73–85. https://doi.org/10.1099/00221287-111-1-73.

"Homo floresiensis: Making Sense of the Small-Bodied Hominin Fossils from Flores." Learn Science at Scitable. https://www.nature.com/scitable/knowledge/library/homo-floresiensis-making-sense-of-the-small-91387735/.

Hoyle, F., & Wickramasinghe, C. *Evolution from Space*. New York: Simon & Shuster, 1981.

Hu, W. et al. "Genomic inference of a severe human bottleneck during the Early to Middle Pleistocene transition." *Science* 381, no. 6661 (August 2023): 979–984. https://doi.org/10.1126/science.abq7487.

Hublin, J. "The prehistory of compassion." *Proceedings of the National Academy of Sciences* 106, no.16 (April 2009): 6429–6430. https://doi.org/10.1073/pnas.0902614106.

Hud, N. V. "Searching for lost nucleotides of the pre-RNA World with a self-refining model of early Earth." *Nature Communications* 9, no. 1 (December 2018). https://doi.org/10.1038/s41467-018-07389-2.

Huttner W.B. et al. "Neocortical neurogenesis in development and evolution-Human-specific features." *J Comp Neurol* 532, no. 2 (February 2024). https://onlinelibrary.wiley.com/doi/full/10.1002/cne.25576.

Ialongo, N., & Lago, G. "A Small Change Revolution: Weight Systems and the Emergence of the First Pan-European Money." *Journal of Archaeological Science* 129, no. 105379 (May 2021). https://doi.org/10.1016/j.jas.2021.105379.

"Intermediate-Range Nuclear Forces Treaty (INF Treaty)." U.S. Department of State. December 8, 1987. https://2009-2017.state.gov/t/avc/trty/102360.htm.

"IPCC Sixth Assessment Report: Figure 2.7." Intergovernmental Panel on Climate Change. https://www.ipcc.ch/report/ar6/wg2/figures/chapter-2/figure-2-007.

Jaziri, A. Y. et al. "Dynamics of the Great Oxidation Event from a 3D Climate Model." *Climate of the Past* 18, no. 10. (October 2022): 2421–2447. https://doi.org/10.5194/cp-18-2421-2022.

Jeffery, N. W. et al. "A First Exploration of Genome Size Diversity in Sponges." *Genome* 56, no. 8 (March 2013): 451–456. https://doi.org/10.1139/gen-2012-0122.

Jonas, K. "Origins: 3.14159265. . ." Biblical Archaeology Society. March 5, 2024. https://www.biblicalarchaeology.org/daily/ancient-cultures/origins-pi/

Jones, H. W. "The Recent Large Reduction in Space Launch Cost." NASA Technical Reports Server (NTRS). July 8, 2018. https://ntrs.nasa.gov/citations/20200001093.

Kamrani, K. "Earliest Known Cave Art Reveals 51,000-Year-Old Storytelling on Indonesian Island." Anthropology.net. July 5, 2024. https://www.anthropology.net/p/earliest-known-cave-art-reveals-51000.

Kazilek. "Insect and Human Biology." Arizona State University. https://askabiologist.asu.edu/insect-and-human-biology.

Kerrod, R. *Encyclopedia of Science Heavens 2*. New York: MacMillian Reference USA, 1978.

Kimball, D. "Nuclear False Warnings and the Risk of Catastrophe." Arms Control Association. December 2019. https://www.armscontrol.org/act/2019-12/focus/nuclear-false-warnings-and-risk-catastrophe.

Kirschvink, J. L. et al. "Paleoproterozoic Snowball Earth: Extreme Climatic and Global Change and Its Biological Consequences." *Proceedings of the National Academy of Sciences* 97, no. 4 (February 2000): 1400–1405. https://doi.org/10.1073/pnas.97.4.1400.

Koch, T. L. "Evolutionary mystery divides scientists: Did the nervous system evolve twice?" ScienceNordic. July 3, 2020. https://shorturl.at/0WyrI.
Kováč, L. "The 20 W Sleep-Walkers." *EMBO Reports* 11, no. 1 (December 2009): 2. https://doi.org/10.1038/embor.2009.266.

Kryśkiewicz, H. "The Parthians – A Worthy Enemy of Rome? Remarks on Roman-Parthian Political Conflict in the Ist c. B.C., and its Influence on Roman Imperial Ideology." *The World of the Orient* 3 (September 2017): 60–72. https://doi.org/10.15407/orientw2017.03.060.

Kurihara, E. et al. "Development of a Functionally Minimized Mutant of the R3C Ligase Ribozyme Offers Insight into the Plausibility of the RNA World Hypothesis." *Biology* 3, no. 3 (July 2014): 452–465. https://doi.org/10.3390/biology3030452.

Larsen, C. S. et al. "Bioarchaeology of Neolithic Çatalhöyük Reveals Fundamental Transitions in Health, Mobility, and Lifestyle in Early Farmers." *Proceedings of the National Academy of Sciences* 116, no. 26 (March 2019): 12615–12623. https://doi.org/10.1073/pnas.1904345116.

Larson, R. B., & Bromm, V. "The First Stars in the Universe." *Scientific American*. December 2001. http://www.astro.yale.edu/larson/papers/SciAm04.pdf.

Ibid. "The First Stars in the Universe." *Scientific American* February 20, 2024. https://shorturl.at/sjE5e.

Li, Y. et al. "Chromosome-Level Reference Genome of the Jellyfish Rhopilema Esculentum." *GigaScience* 9, no. 4 (April 2020). https://doi.org/10.1093/gigascience/giaa036.

Liebeskind, B. J. et al. "Complex Homology and the Evolution of Nervous Systems." *Trends in Ecology & Evolution* 31, no. 2 (February 2016): 127–135. https://doi.org/10.1016/j.tree.2015.12.005.

"LightSail 2 Mission Success." The Planetary Society. November 10, 2020. ttps://www.planetary.org/planetary-report/tpr-2019-3.

Linde, A. "A Brief History of the Multiverse." *arXiv* (December 2015). https://doi.org/10.48550/arxiv.1512.01203.

Loeb, A. "The Habitable Epoch of the Early Universe." *International Journal of Astrobiology* 13, no. 4 (September 2014): 337–339. https://doi.org/10.1017/s1473550414000196.

Lordkipanidze, D. et al. "The Earliest Toothless Hominin Skull." *Nature* 434, no. 7034 (April 2005): 717–718. https://doi.org/10.1038/434717b.
Lukas, D. Archive Reports. Çatalhöyük Research Project. November 23, 2015. https://www.catalhoyuk.com/research/archive_reports.

Maloney, K. "What's Mycelium? The Unbelievable Story of Fungi's Underground Mycelial Network." MUD\WTR. April 24, 2023. https://mudwtr.com/blogs/trends-with-benefits/what-is-mycelium-the-story-of-the-mycelial-network.

Mandal, A. "Virus Origins." News-Medical. June 21, 2023. https://www.news-medical.net/health/Virus-Origins.aspx.

Marineros, A. "History of the Sailing Boat." Alegría Marineros. March 9, 2024. https://alegriamarineros.com/en/sailing-through-time-the-fascinating-history-of-the-sailing-boat/.

Martini, H. "Man's Best Distant Relative: How Much DNA Do We Share with Dogs?" DNA Diagnostics Centre. October 30, 2023. https://dnacentre.co.uk/blog/mans-best-distant-relative-how-much-dna-do-we-share-with-dogs/.

Matsuda, T. et al. "Error Rate and Specificity of Human and Murine DNA Polymerase η." *Journal of Molecular Biology* 312, no. 2 (September 2001): 335–346. https://doi.org/10.1006/jmbi. 2001.4937.

Maugh, T. H., II. "Cacao Was First Used for Alcohol, Study Finds." *Los Angeles Times*, March 2, 2019. ttps://www.latimes.com/archives/la-xpm-2007-nov-13-sci-cacao13-story.html.

Maytin, E. V., & Habener, J. F. "Transcription Factors C/EBPα, C/EBPβ, and CHOP (Gadd153) Expressed During the Differentiation Program of Keratinocytes In Vitro and In Vivo." *Journal of Investigative Dermatology* 110, no. 3 (March 1998): 238–246. https://doi.org/10.1046/j.1523-1747.1998.00123.x.

McGovern, P. E. et al. "Fermented Beverages of Pre- and Proto-Historic China." *Proceedings of the National Academy of Sciences* 101, no. 51 (December 2004): 17593–17598. https://doi.org/10.1073/pnas.0407921102.

McInerney, P. et al. "Error Rate Comparison during Polymerase Chain Reaction by DNA Polymerase." *Molecular Biology International* (August 2014): 1–8. https://doi.org/10.1155/2014/287430.

Metheny, K. B., & Beaudry, M. C. *Archaeology of Food: An Encyclopedia.* Lanham: Rowman & Littlefield, 2015.

Mi, S. et al. "Syncytin is a Captive Retroviral Envelope Protein Involved in Human Placental Morphogenesis." *Nature* 403, no. 6771 (February 2000): 785–789. https://doi.org/10.1038/35001608.

Moelling, K., & Broecker, F. "Viroids and the Origin of Life." *International Journal of Molecular Sciences* 22, no. 7 (2021): 3476. https://doi.org/10.3390/ijms22073476.

Moody, E. R. R. et al. "The Nature of the Last Universal Common Ancestor and Its Impact on the Early Earth System." *Nature Ecology & Evolution* 8, no. 9 (July 2024): 1654–1666. https://doi.org/10.1038/s41559-024-02461-1.

Moore, M. W., & Brumm, A. "Homo Floresiensis and the African Oldowan." In *Vertebrate Paleobiology and Paleoanthroplogy Series – Interdisciplinary Approaches to the Oldowan*, edited by Eric Delson and Stephen G. B. Chester, 61–69. Berlin: Springer Science & Business Media, 2009.

Moroz, L. "Phylogenomics meets neuroscience: How many times might complex brains have evolved?" *Acta Biologica Hungarica* 63, no. 2 (June 2012): 3–19. https://doi.org/10.1556/abiol.63.2012.suppl.2.1.

Munday, J. N. "Tackling Climate Change through Radiative Cooling." *Joule* 3, no. 9 (September 2019): 2057–2060. https://doi.org/10.1016/j.joule.2019.07.010.

Neufeld, M. "Robert Goddard and the First Liquid-Propellant Rocket." National Air and Space Museum. March 16, 2016. https://airandspace.si.edu/stories/editorial/robert-goddard-and-first-liquid-propellant-rocket.

Nielsen, M. "Homo Neanderthalensis and the Evolutionary Origins of Ritual in Homo Sapiens." *Philosophical Transactions of the Royal Society B Biological Sciences* 375, no. 1805 (June 2020). https://doi.org/10.1098/rstb.2019.0424.

Noble, L. M., & Andrianopoulos, A. "Fungal Genes in Context: Genome Architecture Reflects Regulatory Complexity and Function." *Genome Biology and Evolution* 5, no. 7 (July 2013): 1336–1352. https://doi.org/10.1093/gbe/evt077.

"Nuclear Weapons Spending." Center for Arms Control and Non-Proliferation. December 14, 2020. https://armscontrolcenter.org/issues/security-spending/nuclear-weapons-spending/.

Oba, Y. et al. "Uracil in the Carbonaceous Asteroid (162173) Ryugu." *Nature Communications* 14, no. 1 (March 2023). https://doi.org/10.1038/s41467-023-36904-3.

Odenwald, S. "The Planck Era: Imagining Our Infant Universe." *Astronomy Magazine*, May 18, 2023. https://www.astronomy.com/science/the-planck-era-imagining-our-infant-universe/.

Olejarz, J. "The Great Oxygenation Event as a Consequence of Ecological Modulated by Planetary Change." *Nature Communications* 12, no. 1 (June 2021): https://doi.org/10.1038/s41467-021-23286-7.

Osborne, C. P., & Beerling, D. J. "Nature's Green Revolution: The Remarkable Evolutionary Rise of C4 Plants." *Philosophical Transactions of the Royal Society B Biological Sciences* 361, no. 1465 (November 2005): 173–194. https://doi.org/10.1098/rstb.2005.1737.

"Our Solar System's 'Shocking' Origin Story." ScienceDaily. August 17, 2017. https://www.sciencedaily.com/releases/2017/08/170803103134.htm.

"Ozone Layer Recovery is on Track, due to Success of Montreal Protocol." UN News. January 10, 2023. https://news.un.org/en/story/2023/01/1132277.

Parker, J. et al. "Genome-Wide Signatures of Convergent Evolution in Echolocating Mammals." *Nature* 502, no. 7470 (September 2013): 228–231. https://doi.org/10.1038/nature12511.

Peléšková, Š. "Human Emotional Evaluation of Ancestral and Modern Threats: Fear, Disgust, and Anger." *Frontiers in Psychology* 14 (January 2024). https://doi.org/10.3389/fpsyg.2023. 1321053.

Petigura, E. A. "Prevalence of Earth-Size Planets Orbiting Sun-Like Stars." *Proceedings of the National Academy of Sciences* 110, no. 48 (October 2013): 19273–19278. https://doi.org/10.1073/pnas.1319909110.

Petit, J., Morbidelli, A., & Chambers, J. "The Primordial Excitation and Clearing of the Asteroid Belt." *Icarus* 153, no. 2 (October 2001): 338–347. https://doi.org/10.1006/icar.2001.6702.

"Phylum Cnidaria." Lumen Learning. https://courses.lumenlearning.com/suny-wmopen-biology2/chapter/phylum-cnidaria/.

Piani, L. et al. "Earth's Water May Have Been Inherited from Material Similar to Enstatite Chondrite Meteorites." *Science* 369, no. 6507 (August 2020): 1110–1113. https://doi.org/10.1126/science.aba1948.

"Pistol Shrimp and Goby Partnership." Tropical Fish Hobbyist Magazine. https://shorturl.at/gTquQ.

Pontius, J. U. et al. "Initial Sequence and Comparative Analysis of the Cat Genome." *Genome Research* 17, no. 11 (June 2007): 1675–1689. https://doi.org/10.1101/gr.6380007.

Prockter, L. M. "Ice in the Solar System." *Johns Hopkins APL Technical Digest* 26, no. 2 (2005): 175. https://secwww.jhuapl.edu/techdigest/content/techdigest/pdf/V26-N02/26-02-Prockter.pdf.

"Protoistory and History of Beer in Ancient India." Beer Studies. https://beer-studies.com/en/world-history/Birth-of-brewing/Combined-fermented_beverages/Indian-Beer-brewing-bassin.

Pugliese, D. "Canadian Forces Top-Heavy with Generals as Rank and File Shrinks." *Ottawa Citizen.* November 22, 2021. https://ottawacitizen.com/news/national/defence-watch/canadian-forces-top-heavy-with-generals-as-rank-and-file-significantly-shrinks.

Radovčić, D. et al. "Evidence for Neandertal Jewelry: Modified White-Tailed Eagle Claws at Krapina." *PLoS ONE* 10, no. 3 (March 2015). https://doi.org/10.1371/journal.pone.0119802.

Richeson, A. W. "Hypatia of Alexandria." *National Mathematics Magazine* 15, no. 2 (November 1940): 74. https://doi.org/10.2307/3028426.

Riedlberger, P. "Rome and Persia at War, 502-532." Bryn Mawr Classical Review. https://bmcr.brynmawr.edu/1998/1998.11.23/.

Rodhe, H. et al. "Svante Arrhenius and the Greenhouse Effect." *Ambio* 26, no. 1 (February 1997). https://www.jstor.org/stable/4314542.

Rohde, O. et al. "Searching for Our Universal Common Ancestor." *Nature* 431 (September 2004): 518–562. http://www.stat.yale.edu/~jtc5/papers/CommonAncestors/Nature_NewsAndViews.pdf.

Rohde, R. A., & Muller, R. A. "Cycles in fossil diversity." *Nature* 434, no. 7030 (March 2005): 208–210. https://doi.org/10.1038/nature03339.

Rosales, C. "Neutrophil: A Cell with Many Roles in Inflammation or Several Cell Types?" 9 (February 2018). https://doi.org/10.3389/fphys.2018.00113.

Ros-Rocher, N. et al. "The Origin of Animals: An Ancestral Reconstruction of the Unicellular-to-Multicellular Transition." *Open Biology* 11, no. 2 (February 2021). https://doi.org/10.1098/rsob.200359.

Rubin, V. "Dark Matter in the Universe." *University of Pennsylvania Press* 132, no. 4 (December 1988): 434–443. https://www.jstor.org/stable/986963.

Ryanhinck. "Nephite Money was Base 8 (and possibly Jaredite)." Science Is True and the Church Is Too. January 10, 2022. https://shorturl.at/8abtZ.

Sabater, B. "Evolution and Function of the Chloroplast: Current Investigations and Perspectives." *International Journal of Molecular Sciences* 19, no. 10 (October 2018): 3095. https://doi.org/10.3390/ijms19103095.

Sackton, T. B. et al. "Dynamic Evolution of the Innate Immune System in Drosophila." (November 2007): 1461–1468. https://doi.org/10.1038/ng.2007.60.

Sagan, C. *Murmurs of Earth: The Voyager Interstellar Record*. New York: Ballantine Books, 1978.

Sagan, C. et al. "A Message from Earth." *Science* 175, no. 4042 (February 1972): 881–884. https://doi.org/10.1126/science. 175.4024.881.

Samuela, M. "Titiro 'Ētu – Star Peeker." *Titiro 'Ētu – Star Peeker* 67 (2024).

Schultz, D. T. et al. "Ancient gene linkages support ctenophores as sister to other animals." *Nature* 618, no. 7963 (May 2023): 110–117. https://doi.org/10.1038/s41586-023-05936-6.

Schwab, I. R. "The Evolution of Eyes: Major Steps – The Keeler Lecture 2017: Centenary of Keeler Ltd." *Eye* 32, no. 2 (October 2017): 302–313. https://doi.org/10.1038/eye.2017.226.

"Science's Breakthrough of The Year: Illumination Of The Dark, Expanding Universe." ScienceDaily. December 3, 2003. https://www.sciencedaily.com/releases/2003/12/031219073445.htm.

"Scientists Find Smallest Number of Genes Needed for Organism's Survival." ScienceDaily. October 26, 2024. www.sciencedaily.com/releases/1999/12/991213052506.htm

Scott, J. *The Vinyl Frontier: The Story of NASA's Interstellar Mixtape*. London: Bloomsbury Publishing, 2019.

Serganov, A., & Patel, D. J. "Ribozymes, Riboswitches and Beyond: Regulation of Gene Expression Without Proteins." *Nature Reviews Genetics* 8, no. 10 (September 2007): 776–790. https://doi.org/10.1038/nrg2172.

"Shanidar 1." The Smithsonian Institution's Human Origins Program. August 30, 2022. https://humanorigins.si.edu/evidence/human-fossils/fossils/shanidar-1.

Sharov, A. A. "Genome Increase as a Clock for the Origin and Evolution of Life." *Biology Direct* 1, no. 1 (June 2006): 17. https://doi.org/10.1186/1745-6150-1-17.

Silva, L. et al. "Albinism in Plants – Far Beyond the Loss of Chlorophyll: Structural and Physiological Aspects of Wild-Type and Albino Royal Poinciana (Delonix Regia) Seedlings." *Plant Biology* 22, no. 5 (June 2020): 761–768. https://doi.org/10.1111/plb.13146.

Slack, J. M. W. "Metaplasia and Transdifferentiation: from Pure Biology to the Clinic." *Nature Reviews Molecular Cell Biology* 8, no. 5 (March 2007): 369–378. https://doi.org/10.1038/nrm2146.

Sohn, S. et al. "GM-CSF-based Mobilization Effect in Normal Healthy Donors for Allogeneic Peripheral Blood Stem Cell Transplantation." *Bone Marrow Transplantation* 30, no. 2 (July 2002): 81–86. https://doi.org/10.1038/sj.bmt.1703598.

Sorensen, D. W. "The Role of TGF—β Signaling in Cardiomyocyte Proliferation." *Current Heart Failure Reports* 17, no. 5 (July 2020): 225–233. https://doi.org/10.1007/s11897-020-00470-2.

Spencer, D. A. et al. "The LightSail 2 Solar Sailing Mission Summary." Small Satellite Conference. https://digitalcommons.usu.edu/smallsat/2023/all2023/59/.

Springsteen, G. et al. "Linked Cycles of Oxidative Decarboxylation of Glyoxylate as Protometabolic Analogs of the Citric Acid Cycle." *Nature Communications* 9, no. 1 (January 2018). https://doi.org/10.1038/s41467-017-02591-0.

"The Early Universe." University of Oregon. https://pages.uoregon.edu/jimbrau/astr123/Notes/Chapter27.html.

"The Gaia Sausage: The Major Collision that Changed the Milky Way Galaxy." Carnegie Mellon University News. July 4, 2018. https://www.cmu.edu/news/stories/archives/2018/july/gaia-sausage.html.

"The Great Dying." NASA Science. https://science.nasa.gov/science-research/earth-science/the-great-dying/.

"The Great Inca Rituals and the Maize Beer." Beer Studies. https://beer-studies.com/en/world-history/First-empires/Inca-Empire/Inca-rituals-maize-beer.

"The Matter-Antimatter Asymmetry Problem." CERN. October 11, 2024. https://home.cern/science/physics/matter-antimatter-asymmetry-problem.

"The Montreal Protocol on Substances that Deplete the Ozone Layer." Ozone Secretariat. https://ozone.unep.org/treaties/montreal-protocol.

"The Nobel Prize in Physics 2019." NobelPrize.org. https://www.nobelprize.org/prizes/physics/2019/press-release/.

Tian, N. et al. "Trends in World Military Expenditure, 2023." SIPRI (April 2024). https://doi.org/10.55163/bqga2180.

"Tiny sea creatures reveal the ancient origins of neurons." ScienceDaily. September 23, 2023. https://www.sciencedaily.com/releases/2023/09/230919154832.htm.

"Treaty on the Prohibition of Nuclear Weapons." United Nations Office for Disarmament Affairs. https://shorturl.at/1kCe4.

Tuchow, N. W., & Wright, J. T. "The Abundance of Belatedly Habitable Planets and Ambiguities in Definitions of the Continuously Habitable Zone." *arXiv* (January 2023). https://doi.org/10.48550/arxiv.2301.02961.

Ulrich, A. "Ndom numbers." Of Languages and Numbers. https://www.languagesandnumbers.com/how-to-count-in-ndom/en/nqm/.

"Understanding Human Genetic Variation." National Institutes of Health: National Library of Medicine. https://shorturl.at/dGnKv.

Van De Mieroop, M. *A History of the Ancient Near East ca. 3000–323 BC.* New Jersey: Wiley-Blackwell, 2006.

Van, P. T. et al. "First Annotated Draft Genomes of Nonmarine Ostracods (Ostracoda, Crustacea) with Different Reproductive Modes." *G3 Genes Genomes Genetics* 11, no. 4 (April 2021). https://doi.org/10.1093/g3journal/jkab043.

Vasas, V. et al. "Evolution Before Genes." *Biology Direct* 7, no. 1 (January 2012). https://doi.org/10.1186/1745-6150-7-1.

Villa, P. et al. "Border Cave and the beginning of the Later Stone Age in South Africa." *Proceedings of the National Academy of Sciences* 109, no. 33 (July 2012): 13208–13213. https://doi.org/10.1073/pnas.1202629109.

Wang, D. Y. et al. "Divergence Time Estimates for the Early History of Animal Phyla and the Origin of Plants, Animals and Fungi." *Proceedings of the Royal Society B: Biological Sciences* 266, no. 1415 (January 1999): 163–171. https://doi.org/10.1098/rspb.1999.0617.

Wang, J. et al. "Early Evidence for Beer Drinking in a 9000-year-old Platform Mound in Southern China." *PLoS ONE* 16, no. 8 (August 2021). https://doi.org/10.1371/journal.pone.0255833.

Williams, J. et al. "Solar Farm Fact Sheet." IEEE. https://shorturl.at/n80aL.

Wolchover, N. "A New Physics Theory of Life." Quanta Magazine. January 22, 2014. https://www.quantamagazine.org/a-new-thermodynamics-theory-of-the-origin-of-life-20140122/.

Wu, W., & Liu, Y. "Radiation Entropy Flux and Entropy Production of the Earth system." *Reviews of Geophysics* 48, no. 2 (June 2010). https://doi.org/10.1029/2008rg000275.

X, S. "Milky Way Churns Out Seven New Stars Per Year, Scientists Say." *Phys.org*. January 5, 2006. https://phys.org/news/2006-01-milky-churns-stars-year-scientists.html.

Yusufoglu, Y. et al. "Improving performance of household refrigerators by incorporating phase change materials." *International Journal of Refrigeration* 57 (September 2015): 173–185. https://doi.org/10.1016/j.ijrefrig.2015.04.020.

Zaitsev, A. & Ignatov, S. "Report on Cosmic Call 1999." CP Lire. http://www.cplire.ru/html/ra&sr/irm/report-1999.html.

Zhu, R. "New evidence on the earliest human presence at high northern latitudes in northeast Asia." *Nature* 431, no. 7008 (September 2004): 559–562. https://doi.org/10.1038/nature02829.

Books for Young People from Linda Leith Publishing

ABC MTL
Jeanne Painchaud, illus. Bruno Ricca, trans. Katia Grubisic. 2019.
Non-fiction/Montreal; 3 to 14 years; ISBN: 9781773900353.

Little Girl Gazelle
Stéphane Martelly, illus. Albin Christen; trans. Katia Grubisic, 2020.
Fiction 4 to 8 years; ISBN: 9781773900711.

Dear Humans: A Letter from the Animals
Nisha Coleman, illus. Shanthony Exum, 2022.
Non-fiction/Climate Change; 4 to 8 years; ISBN: 9781773901312.

Cosmic Wonder: Our Place in the Epic Story of the Universe
Written and illustrated by Nathan Hellner-Mestelman, 2024.
YA Non-fiction/Science & Technology/Astronomy; 14 to 18 years;
ISBN: 9781773901596.

Miss Matty
Edeet Ravel, illus. Steven Stowell, 2025.
YA Novel/World War II/Montreal; 14 to 18 years; ISBN: 9781773901657.

The Language of the Stars:
The Scientific Story of a Few Billion Years in a Few Hundred Pages
Written and illustrated by Nathan Hellner-Mestelman, 2025.
YA Non-fiction/Science & Technology/Astronomy; 14 to 18 years;
ISBN: 9781773901718.

Christmas Weekend
Monique Polak, 2025.
YA Fiction/Family/Action & Adventure; 12 to 18 years;
ISBN: 9781773901770.